HOLY LAND?

HOLY LAND?

Challenging questions from
the biblical landscape

Andrew D. Mayes

First published in Great Britain in 2011

Society for Promoting Christian Knowledge
36 Causton Street
London SW1P 4ST
www.spckpublishing.co.uk

British Library Cataloguing-in-Publication Data
A catalogue record for this book is available from the British Library

ISBN 978–0–281–06466–3
eBook ISBN 978–0–281–06657–5

Typeset by Graphicraft Ltd, Hong Kong
First printed in Great Britain by Ashford Colour Press
Subsequently digitally printed in Great Britain

Produced on paper from sustainable forests

Contents

Illustrations

———•◆•———

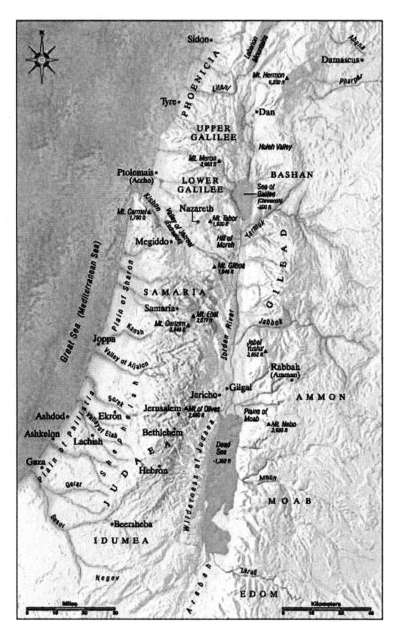

The Holy Land in biblical times

Introduction

———•◆•———

The terrain of the Holy Land is a questioning landscape, in more than one sense. It poses to us acute questions which touch on the deepest issues of human life. It invites us to ask our own questions. Written in Jerusalem, this book aims to help the reader to discover the topography of the Holy Land afresh, and let the land speak its contemporary and timeless questions to us. As Director of Courses for St George's College, leading a variety of pilgrimage-journeys in the lands of the Bible for students from all over the world, I realized that pilgrims need support in order to tease out the questions which the land poses today, and the present book emerges from this setting. It is offered not as an answer book but as a resource book: the material will help you work through your own responses to the questions.

The landscape of the Holy Land is one of vivid contrasts. The very shape of the land has been formed by the grating movement along fault lines, seismic shifts and clashes between tectonic plates in the Great Rift Valley of the Jordan: a clue, an indicator to us that this might turn out to be a land where conflict is endemic, where different sorts of masses meet and interact, where fault lines are to be detected within human society itself. This land-bridge between Egypt and Mesopotamia, this meeting place between Africa, Asia and Europe, has since antiquity been a place of encounter and clash. Here, where the desert and the sea face each other, where the bleak Dead Sea in the lowest place on earth is linked to the teeming and life-giving Sea of Galilee, where wilderness and fertility lie side by side, is a land of paradoxes, contradictions and deeply challenging questions.

Thus the starting point for our reflections in this book is the landscape itself, which becomes a catalyst for thinking about a range of issues which are both urgent and abiding. This approach is inspired, first of all, by the prophetic and metaphorical approach to creation that we see in the Scriptures. Topography suggests typology. The Psalms delight in the symbolism of trees, water, rock, mountain and wind (Pss. 1; 18). Every prophet of the land exults in vivid images from the hills: the very terrain speaks the message. Isaiah cries out: 'Every valley shall be lifted up, and every mountain and hill be made low' (Isa. 40.4). Hosea sees climate and field as bespeaking God: 'Sow for yourselves righteousness; reap steadfast love; break up your fallow ground; for it is time to seek the LORD, that he may come and rain righteousness upon you' (Hos. 10.12). Amos pleads: 'Let justice roll down like waters, and righteousness like an ever-flowing stream' (Amos 5.24). The prophets draw from the land powerful metaphors for salvation and judgement, and the contours of the terrain become a symbolic universe. Jesus himself takes a deeply contemplative and sacramental approach to the land, the secrets of the kingdom revealing themselves through parables of seed, mountain, field and sea (Matt. 13; Mark 11.23). Today, this same land is both holy and unholy: it is at once a sacred landscape and a scarred landscape. At every point ancient biblical memories collide with modern political and social realities. The very topography poses to us questions and dilemmas that will help us as we traverse the terrain of our own spiritual journey, wherever in the world we may be living.

The approach of the book is, second, inspired by the conviction that spirituality and physicality are interwoven and inseparable. While the landscape raises for us issues that touch on our life in the Spirit, it also requires us to look again at our life as incarnate and embodied: we will face questions that link us to the divine–human communion, but also require us to attend to our life in society today. Time and eternity meet here, sometimes uncomfortably. One striking feature of pilgrimage to the Holy Land is the constant juxtaposition between spiritual opportunities and present-day political and social contexts: in almost every 'holy place' there is an unsettling reminder of contemporary realities. The pilgrim can never escape into a 'spiritual moment' untouched by demanding questions, but at every turn must expect spirituality to be confronted and challenged by today's pain and hope, and so must be prepared to experience an interplay or dialogue with issues of justice and peace. This book thus invites us into a dynamic arising from the land itself, in which we seek to attend to the voices of the peoples, the insights of spiritual writers, and the call of the gospel.

This book is offered to three types of reader. First, it is for those who are planning to go to the Holy Land on pilgrimage. You will be wanting to prepare for your adventure, and the book will awaken and alert you to the profound issues that await you, enabling you to begin to prayerfully grapple and wrestle with these. Sometimes pilgrimages turn out to be, unintentionally, superficial: thanks to the constraints of time, or perhaps to narrowness of vision, pilgrims find themselves running where Jesus walked. Sometimes pilgrimages can be purely devotional or historical in focus and fail to engage with the Holy Land as it is today. My aim is to enable you to undertake a pilgrimage that will be profound and life-changing as it interacts with the challenges of the land.

A second group of readers will be those who have visited the Holy Land already. You long to revisit it in your memory or imagination, not only to recall treasured moments, but also to revisit it in a deeper sense – taking another look, thinking afresh about its questions. A third group includes those who may for various reasons not be able to visit the Holy Land. You will want to see how the land of the Bible can inspire Christian discipleship today.

The issues here are not parochial but universal – they are rooted and contextualized but they invite you to work out responses in your own setting. *Holy Land?* looks at issues that are indispensable for anyone on a journey of faith. Each chapter explores one major theme and identifies questions that emerge. In the opening chapter, the city asks us, What is home? In Chapter 2, the land invites us to consider the issue of holiness and the question, Where can I find God? From the waters of the River Jordan, in Chapter 3, questions relating to the theme of identity bubble up: Who am I? In Chapter 4, we enter the depths and discover the significance of caves in the landscape, asking: How can I face the darkness? Chapter 5 introduces us to significant rocks, which confront us with issues of memory and forgiveness, while in Chapter 6, we ascend the Mount of Transfiguration and look at the issue of control and letting go. The water of the Sea of Galilee, in Chapter 7, invites us to explore the issue of the sharing of scarce resources. In Chapter 8, we enter three very different gardens which in their different ways speak of the theme of struggle. Our exploration of the desert in Chapter 9 demands that we face the questions about solitude and silence. In Chapters 10 and 11, we attend to aspects of the human landscape, receiving the questions of the walls and roads of the land. Finally, in Chapter 12, the sea invites us to look out to wider horizons and consider our vocation and mission.

The book may be used by individuals or groups – questions for reflection are suggested at the end of each chapter. It may be used by parish pilgrimage groups upon their return from the Holy Land, in order to take their thinking to a deeper level, as a tool for theological reflection. It may be used by groups preparing for pilgrimage, to open heart and mind to the issues that await them. It may be used by a Lenten or parish study group as a resource to deepen their discipleship.

I am grateful to all who have made this book possible: to my wife, Ann; to SPCK editor Alison Barr; and to colleagues and pilgrims at St George's College, especially Rod Jepsen, the chaplain, who contributed many of the photographs (that in Chapter 4 is by Ben Drury). I hope that this exploration will enable you to discover the Holy Land in a fresh way, and help you engage anew with your own land and context.

Andrew D. Mayes
St George's College Jerusalem

*Figure 1 Fresh Israeli settlements in an Arab neighbourhood face
the locale of God's house, the Dome of the Rock*

1

The city's questions

What is home?

I kiss the walls at Damascus Gate every time I get back to Jerusalem. This is one of the wonders of the world! The sights, the smells, but most of all the holy places invigorate me. Whatever happens, we are going to stay here. Of course we could sell up and move out to Ramallah – it is fast becoming the capital for Palestinians – but we are not going to let them do what they did to my family in Acco [Acre] – throw us out. Of course I am tempted as a young man to make a career in Dubai, like some of my friends. But *this* is home. Of course I get upset by the Israeli settlers taking our Arab properties in the city – their flags and their spitting at us. By staying put in Jerusalem we maintain our dignity. Things are not good here for young people right now.

Abed, 22, works on Jerusalem's Via Dolorosa at his dad's shop, which is crammed with traditional items, including antique Arab women's headdresses and wedding robes. He studies business at the Arab American University at Jenin and comes to help a couple of days each week. Around the corner is a building bedecked with large Israeli flags, the Star of David blowing defiantly in the breeze. Above an archway a sign reads *Igud Lohamay*, denoting the Association of the Fighters of the Battle for Jerusalem. In 1967 a group of soldiers regained possession of this building from the Jordanians; having served from 1886 until the Arab uprising in 1936 as a Jewish college for the study of the Torah, once again it functions today as a yeshiva. A Zionist sister organization, *Ateret Kohanim* (literally 'Crown of Priests'), is dedicated to acquiring

1

Arab properties in the Old City and in East Jerusalem, so as to accomplish the Judaizing of the city.

A narrow courtyard off the street is packed with motor scooters and bicycles and a flight of steps leads to a buzzing, hectic scene, for it is the end of breakfast for the yeshiva, and the landing serves as both corridor and kitchen. Already students are in the main room, which is at the same time dining room, synagogue – with the ark for the Torah scrolls and bema, from where the Scriptures are read – and study room, crammed with desks and chairs. The seminary has more than two hundred students, mainly in their twenties, from all over Israel: some hope to go on to become rabbis, while others will follow professions in the military, law or business. When the yeshiva was re-established, the focus was on studying temple ritual – in the hope that the Third Temple would be rebuilt within a generation, as the necessary precursor to the coming of the Messiah.

Asaph, 23, is earnest and intense and cautious of visitors but gently soft-spoken, and courteous. He explains:

We are here to study Torah, Halakah [Regulations], Talmud [rabbinic teaching] and Gemara [commentaries] – just like other yeshivot. We are able to put off entering the army, the Israeli Defence Forces, because Torah study can take precedence over everything else. I get an exemption certificate each year from the Dean to show to the army authorities, so they can't call me up. Of course, it is the greatest privilege living so close to the Temple Mount and the Kotel [Western Wall], but it is mingled with the everyday reality. This is a hostile environment, a scary street to live on. A rabbi from here was stabbed in the neck a couple of years ago. He survived. There was a murder before that. Arabs sometimes spit at us going down to the Kotel, or speak abuse. You can't trust people. I am always wary. I look at people closely as I walk down, in case they might attack me – you learn to stay very alert. For us, fear is in the air. It is a risky thing for Jews to live here. We do not say we live in the Muslim quarter – we call it the renewed Jewish quarter. It is part of the restoration of Israel, the redemption of the land, the

Jewish people back on this soil. You ask me what I think of my Arab neighbours – I can't make a reply. But this is sure: we are back on the street. It is a restoration. We are reclaiming this street for the Jews. We are here to stay!

Almost next door lives an Armenian Christian, Katar, who came to Jerusalem 15 years ago to marry a man from an old Jerusalemite family: they have two daughters.

My grandmother was exiled and made a refugee twice. First, after seeing with her own eyes the killings of fellow Armenians in Turkey, in 1915 she fled with her parents to Jaffa, the Mediterranean port of Palestine. There she grew up, and married my grandfather. At the age of 39, in 1948, she fled again from Jaffa as all the Palestinian and Armenian families had to move out, and she came to Jordan with thousands of other refugees. I really feel for the Palestinians. They suffer like the Armenians suffered. I mean, there are things in common. Being displaced, insecure, uncertain. I feel a certain connection with them. How is it like living here? I feel I don't really belong in a way, though I live here.

Where is home for me? I am swinging between two worlds, between Jordan and Armenia. My story is there. This is not my country. This is the only Christian convent on this part of the road: this is the Muslim quarter, we have Muslim neighbours. At first, I found the presence of Israeli soldiers on the street here unnerving. I mean, in Jordan, where you see soldiers you expect to see trouble: that is why they are there. Here it is normal, everyday. It always reminds you that we are under military occupation. We have to try to live a normal life in a place which is never normal! And as a mother, I always feel protective towards my girls. I fear for the safety of my girls. We live an enclosed life. We Armenians have to keep separate, to preserve our identity and our culture, that is how we survive. We speak the Armenian language in the family, and I don't let the girls out to play in the street with the Arab children.

These three voices, Muslim, Jewish and Christian, from present-day Jerusalem encapsulate hopes and fears which cluster around the theme of 'home' – the theme we are exploring in this opening chapter. The Old City of Jerusalem, just one square kilometre in area, is home to some forty thousand people: Jews, Christians and Muslims, living cheek by jowl.

As one crosses the threshold of the city, the senses are assaulted. There is a cacophony of sound: church bells pealing out, the five-times-daily call to prayer from the minarets, a siren blast at Friday sundown announcing the arrival of the Jewish Sabbath, while sellers cry out their bargains, beggars call out for alms and playing children shriek. A diversity of fragrances fills the air: early morning bakeries emit their intoxicating smell of newly baked bread; Arab women, coming in from the countryside, sit in the gutter to sell aromatic freshly picked mint, thyme and sage; spices such as cumin, cloves, cinnamon and saffron are piled high at open stalls. The smell of roasting kebabs competes with the sweet allure of pastries. A riot of colour hits the eye: crimson-red pomegranates, green olives and bright yellow mangoes overspill their stalls, while stunning embroidered carpets bedeck the alleyways. The city is alive and effervescent with energy: mingling and blending together in the paradox of the holy city are the people's heartaches and hopes, aspirations and anguishes. It is a veritable melting pot of cultures, a fractured mosaic of humanity. Jerusalem is an ever-changing kaleidoscope, a matrix of faiths, a vortex of devotion, a religious maelstrom, a microcosm of the world.

The four crowded residential quarters are home to diverse communities, each with its own distinctive character. The golden Dome of the Rock, resplendent in the sunshine, dominates the Muslim quarter and is glimpsed at various turns from the alleys. The area heaves with humanity, vibrant with its mosques and markets, its shops selling everything from copies of the Qur'an to dustpans. The streets are a human sea, with a tide that ebbs and flows according to the hours of prayer at the Al Aqsa mosque, as men flood up to the Noble Sanctuary (the Temple Mount) to perform their devotions in response to the call of the muezzin, and back again to their homes. Ancient men sit smoking hubble-bubbles, while young men call out their wares.

Homes are built on level after level: above the bustle of the narrow lanes and the dark, arched passageways rises a whole neighbourhood of town-houses and flats, often in stone Ottoman-period buildings, crumbling with age, that may preserve Crusader or Mamluke architectural remnants. Chronic overcrowding creates its own stresses: there may be ten people crammed into a room, as permission is rarely given for extensions to be built, even though the birth rate is high.

For the children, life takes place in the street. There is precious little physical space for them to grow up in: they can't do normal childhood things, like sitting down in the house and doing art, or having a story read to them because the space is too tiny and too full. So the children have to live in the warren of the streets – a great place for hide and seek, but hardly convenient for ever-popular football. They live a restricted life, and there are always security cameras watching them. They lack many of the elements essential to 'being at home'; there is little sense of personal security – security in themselves. They pick up anxiety and fear from their parents, who are stressed because of high unemployment and poverty. Parents get frustrated and snappy and take their frustrations out on the children. Domestic violence is a problem, and it is normal for parents to slap their children. They see it as building strength in the kids. The sense of overcrowding at home and restlessness on the streets is compounded by the fact that, due to under-funding, there is a shortfall of 1,000 classrooms in East Jerusalem; according to a recent report, 14,500 Arab children of school age do not, or cannot, attend school.[1]

The Armenian quarter is a different world. A silent monastic compound centring on the shrine of St James' cathedral, it is peopled by monk-priests, seminarians and the elderly: about 1,500 live in a place which accounts for a sixth of the city's area. The Armenian community has been here since the fourth century, as the quarter has been a place both of pilgrimage for the first Christian nation and of refuge from the land of Armenia, often overrun throughout history by armies and invaders. Children are few, and the place has a tranquillity unknown anywhere else in the city.

Next door, the Jewish quarter faces the Western Wall, the last remnant of the Temple, which pulsates with the *davening* of the Orthodox, rolling rhythmically backwards and forwards as they recite the Psalms. Their quarter is a sterile-clean, freshly swept environment filled with new, up-market apartments, all built since the Israeli occupation of 1967. The crisp straight-lined walls of the new buildings, with their gleaming stone, contrast with the ragged and worn dwellings found elsewhere in the city. Many are owned by wealthy but absentee American Jews. There is a substantial student population and many yeshivas and synagogues. Rare splashes of greenery and open spaces help create a calmer environment for the residents.

The Christian quarter is a labyrinth of streets, bearing witness to Chesterton's remark that Jerusalem is a 'city of staircases', for here flights of steps lead to the highest part of the city. The streets are choked with homes, many owned by the Greek or Catholic Church and let out at low rents to poor working families. The imposing residences of the Latin and Greek Patriarchs contrast with the modest cells of the monastic communities, hidden from sight behind closed doors but thriving around an open courtyard, each with its own chapel. This area is served by Church-run clinics and day centres for the elderly, while for the young there are vibrant schools and halls for the popular scouts. Shops close to the Church of the Resurrection, the Holy Sepulchre, sell every conceivable religious item to cater for a multi-faith market: menorahs stand next to crucifixes, while the Jewish ram's horn trumpet, the *shofar*, lies amid icons and rosaries.

But while the Old City is home to such diverse communities, it is also, in a sense, spiritual home to the world. Pilgrims of all nationalities throng the congested streets: raucous Spaniards with their guitars; noisy and excited Nigerians with their bright, bright clothes; subdued Russian pilgrims, black-cassocked and earnest; joyous and intense Koreans, jostling with photo-taking Japanese. Jewish pilgrims include Birthright-Israel teenagers from America visiting on sponsored trips to help them connect with their Judaistic heritage in the city. Muslims come from India to make their *hajj* to the Dome of the Rock, wearing the white robes of pilgrims. All the world feels at home here: pilgrims experience an indescribable sense of belonging, of homecoming. The residents are open-hearted and welcoming. But deep fears are in the air, fears which shatter any sense that this is 'home sweet home'.

Just outside the city walls, homebuilding and house demolitions mark the story of Jerusalem today. Around the Old City a massive construction programme goes on relentlessly, as the Israeli authorities continue to build Jewish settlements and housing estates, surrounding the city on all sides, on land appropriated from Palestinians, who are forcibly removed, without any compensation. To the east of Jerusalem, on the edge of the Judaean desert, the new settlement of Ma'ale Adummin covers 35 square kilometres of Palestinian territory and has a population of nearly forty thousand Jews. To the north of the city, the long-established Arab community of Sheikh Jarrah, established by Palestinian refugees fleeing the newly created Israeli state in 1948, has experienced a string of house demolitions. Arab dwellings are bulldozed into dust, on the grounds that the legal permissions for their roof or side extensions are not in place; such permits are rarely issued, and overcrowding means that Palestinians must build upwards as families grow. In East Jerusalem and the West Bank 133 homes were demolished by the Israeli authorities in 2010, making 600 people homeless, half of them children.[2] Regularly we hear of house evictions in Jerusalem – Palestinian families thrown out of their homes as Jewish settlers, perhaps with Ottoman-period deeds, claim ownership and move in. The chattels of the departing Arab family are dumped unceremoniously on the street, and within minutes settlers arrive to unpack their removal vans, under the watchful eye of the army. South of Jerusalem's historic city wall, part of the Arab village of Silwan has recently been renamed 'City of David'. Where Arab residents have been expelled from their ancestral homes, the reputed site of David's palace has been identified, by archaeologists funded by the extremist Jewish settler organization Elad. Here the words 'there's no place like home' are bitter-sweet. Arab residents live in fear, wondering which home will be next to receive the door-knock from the soldiers announcing eviction, while Jewish residents in the City of David also live in fear, barricaded within their apartments, many of which have a personal security guard and private surveillance cameras.

Jerusalem, the Holy City, in biblical tradition the actual dwelling place of God, raises acute questions about what is truly home. The very concept of home and homeland evokes the image of living in freedom, dignity and fulfilment: can this be possible in the Holy Land itself?

Seeking a homeland

The search for a Jewish homeland begins with Abraham, in perhaps 2000 BC. God's words come to him at his home in Haran (south-east Turkey): 'Go from your country and your kindred and your father's house to the land that I will show you' (Gen. 12.1). Abraham's journey leads him to Canaan and he receives the promise of land (Gen. 13.14–18). But his descendants are to migrate to Egypt and it is not until the coming of Moses and the great Exodus event (1250 BC) that the Israelites enter the land, under Joshua's leadership. There are two accounts of the advent into the territory in the Old Testament: the book of Joshua tells of a rapid and dramatic takeover of the land, a mighty conquest achieved by the destruction of the locals, while the book of Judges suggests the more gradual migration of a people who need to co-exist with the indigenous inhabitants.

The experience of *galut*, exile, of becoming homeless and enduring the status of refugees, repeats itself in the history of Israel. In 722 BC the northern tribes are taken off into exile by Assyria, never to return; in 586 the Babylonians take a large part of the remaining population into a seventy-year exile. As kingdoms come and go in the Holy Land, the experience of diaspora or scattering is repeated – Jews are expelled from the Holy City in AD 70 and 135, and during the Crusades – and Jewish communities establish themselves through the centuries across the world.

Where then is home? With the advent of Zionism, Jews looked to the establishment of a homeland in Palestine. This desire intensified towards the end of the nineteenth century against a background of Western anti-Semitism, as the sense grew among the Jewish people that they were not 'at home' in places in Europe where they had been long settled. Viewing Palestine as an 'empty' land and failing to recognize the Palestinian Arabs as a people, the watchword of the Jewish people became 'A land without a people for a people without a land'. Britain's 1917 Balfour Declaration, with its support of 'the establishment in Palestine of a national home for the Jewish people', raised hopes of a Zionist state.

The founding of the State of Israel in 1948 was achieved through the destruction or evacuation of 400 Palestinian villages, making 700,000 Palestinians homeless refugees as they fled to the West Bank or to Jordan. Ilan Pappe, former Israeli Professor of History, is among those to have called this 'the ethnic cleansing of Palestine'.[3] In 1950 the Knesset passed the Law of Return, enshrining the *aliyah*: the right of every Jew in the world to return to the country as a resident. Since the Six Day War of 1967 the whole territory from the Mediterranean Sea to the River Jordan has been regarded as the Land of Israel; the occupied West Bank of the Jordan is called by Israelis Judaea and Samaria. One of the first actions of the occupation was the massive destruction of Arab homes – 400 homes of the Moroccan quarter were demolished in 1967, in order to create a piazza for prayer in front of the Western Wall.

Thus the search for a Jewish homeland has entailed the creation of homelessness and exile for many Palestinians. Today over four million Palestinian refugees are registered with the United Nations, a number which includes the children of those displaced and fleeing their homes in 1948 or 1967. In some of their narratives, Arabs trace their presence in the land to the Canaanites them-selves.[4] Certainly, with the Arab conquest in the seventh century, the incoming Arabs intermarried with existing populations, uniting with their long histories in the land. A deep sense of belonging to the earth is represented in the symbol of the olive tree – grown on ancestral lands as a source of food and oil, its roots going deep into the soil – yet today thousands of Palestinian olive trees have been uprooted by Jewish settlers on the West Bank or destroyed by the construction of the Wall. Today many Palestinians feel that they are living as exiles in their own land, prevented by the divisive Separation Barrier from moving freely to visit relatives' homes. Many in East Jerusalem fear that their homes will be next for demolition or eviction. There is a deep sense of not being 'at home' in their residences as there is little sense of personal or familial security or unthreatened permanence. Across the West Bank, there is deep nostalgia and longing for homes from which Palestinians were evicted at gunpoint in 1948. For many, a poignant symbol of their displacement is the key: families treasure the rusting key to their former home, which today may be long-demolished or inhabited by Israelis – a key which they will never be able to use again, but which endures as a sad memento of a family home lost for ever.

Biblical explorations

The theme of God's own dwelling place runs throughout Scripture. At first, there is resistance to the idea of localizing the divine in a house, as the pilgrim God says to David via the prophet Nathan: 'I have not lived in a house since the day I brought up the people of Israel from Egypt to this day, but I have been moving about in a tent and a tabernacle. Wherever I have moved about among all the people of Israel, did I ever speak . . . saying, "Why have you not built me a house of cedar?"' (2 Sam. 7.6, 7). But with the building of the first Temple, and the placing of the Ark of the Covenant within the Holy of Holies, the Psalms celebrate God's homecoming and his dwelling in the midst of the people: 'How lovely is your dwelling-place, O LORD of hosts!' (Ps. 84.1); 'His abode has been established in Salem, his dwelling-place in Zion' (Ps. 76.2). Solomon himself acknowledges a paradox and asks the unanswerable question: 'But will God indeed dwell on the earth? Even heaven and the highest heaven cannot contain you, much less this house that I have built!' (1 Kings 8.27).

Some Psalms celebrate God's omnipresence, even in the darkest places of the earth:

> Where can I go from your spirit?
> Or where can I flee from your presence?
> If I ascend to heaven, you are there;

if I make my bed in Sheol, you are there.
If I take the wings of the morning
and settle at the farthest limits of the sea,
even there your hand shall lead me,
and your right hand shall hold me fast.

(Ps. 139.7–10)

Indeed, the prophets declare that God cannot be confined to a house of brick and mortar. Isaiah insists: 'For thus says the high and lofty one who inhabits eternity, whose name is Holy: I dwell in the high and holy place, and also with those who are contrite and humble in spirit' (Isa. 57.15). The prophets also testify to the shekinah glory and presence of God departing from the Temple building, as a response to idolatry and injustice (Ezek. 11.22, 23).

With the coming of Jesus, God establishes his tabernacle in a new place: 'And the Word became flesh and lived among us' (John 1.14). Indeed, in the perspective of the Gospels, Jesus is the new Temple itself (John 2.13–22). Paul takes this further when he asks: 'Do you not know that you are God's temple, and that God's Spirit dwells in you?' (1 Cor. 3.16). In John's Gospel, the persons of the Holy Trinity seek a dwelling place in the hearts of men and women: 'And I will ask the Father, and he will give you another Advocate, to be with you for ever. This is the Spirit of truth . . . Those who love me will keep my word, and my Father will love them, and we will come to them and make our home with them' (John 14.16, 17a, 23). Conversely, the Christian is to dwell in Christ: 'Abide in me as I abide in you' (John 15.4). Is it possible to live on this earth without a physical home and yet dwell rooted in God in this way?

Certainly the Gospels stress that Jesus was homeless. In Matthew, the infant Jesus becomes a refugee at a few days old as he flees Herod's destruction (Matt. 2.13–15). Later, he leaves Nazareth, his home town, where he is not accepted (Mark 6.1–6). Recent studies have emphasized the itinerancy of Jesus: he is on the road, not setting up a base for operations.[5] Jesus is emphatic: 'Foxes have holes, and birds of the air have nests; but the Son of Man has nowhere to lay his head' (Matt. 8.20). Jesus lives as a pilgrim, in vulnerability and radical trust in God. He is exposed to the elements and to dangers. He encourages his disciples to travel light with few possessions (Luke 10.1–11). Jesus himself enjoys the hospitality of home at Bethany and elsewhere (Matt. 26.6; Mark 11.11; John 12.1). In his parable of the Prodigal Son, homecoming becomes a symbol of salvation (Luke 15) and he brings salvation to the house of Zacchaeus (Luke 19.10). The theme of the house seems particularly significant in Matthew's Gospel,[6] while in Luke a recurring symbol of the inclusive nature of God's kingdom is table fellowship open to all (see, for example, ch. 14).

The Letter to the Hebrews presents Jesus as a pilgrim between earth and heaven, the pioneer and forerunner to heaven. The heavenly Jerusalem is, in a true sense, our true home. As Paul puts it: 'Our citizenship is in heaven' (Phil. 3.20). The Bible ends with a vision of the heavenly Jerusalem and a loud voice crying from God's throne:

> See, the home of God is among mortals.
> He will dwell with them;
> they will be his peoples,
> and God himself will be with them.   (Rev. 21.3)

But the Psalms preserve a hope that even the earthly Jerusalem can be a place where all can belong. Psalm 87 gives us a vision of an inclusive city, with space for all: a place where former enemies live side by side; a place that is birthplace and home to all:

> On the holy mount stands the city he founded;
> the LORD loves the gates of Zion
> more than all the dwellings of Jacob.
> Glorious things are spoken of you,
> O city of God.
> Among those who know me I mention Rahab [Egypt]
>   and Babylon;
> Philistia too, and Tyre, with Ethiopia –
> 'This one was born there,' they say.
> And of Zion it shall be said,

'This one and that one were born in it';
for the Most High himself will establish it.
The LORD records, as he registers the peoples,
'This one was born there.'
Singers and dancers alike say,
'All my springs are in you.'

Questions for reflection

1 What is your experience of home? What is your definition of home? Where can you truly be 'at home'?
2 How do you understand God himself as a pilgrim?
3 In what sense is God our true dwelling place and our heart's true home? To what extent do you feel that the Christian experience is about making space in our lives that God may make his home in us?
4 In what ways can you live as a pilgrim in your society while being home based?
5 How can you live in solidarity with the homeless of the earth while living in comfort and security?

For further reading

K. Armstrong, *One City, Three Faiths* (New York: Alfred A. Knopf, 1996)
C. Chapman, *Whose Promised Land?* (Oxford: Lion, 1992)
D. Cohn-Sherbok and D. El-Alami, *The Palestine-Israeli Conflict: A Beginner's Guide* (Oxford: Oneworld, 2001)
A. M. Eisen, *Galut: Modern Jewish Reflection on Homelessness and Homecoming* (Bloomington & Indianapolis, IN: Indiana University Press, 1986)
A. Qleibo, *Jerusalem in the Heart* (Jerusalem: Kloreus Publications, 2000)

Figure 2 Holy places: localizing the divine? Invitation or warning?

2

The land's questions
What is holy?

———◆◆◆———

The 'Holy Land' – the very name evokes images of a land graced by the presence and revelation of God, a land of 'holy places' where we can encounter God powerfully. But the 'Holy Land' is also a place of contradiction, ambiguity and paradox – it is often rendered unholy today by its oppressions. Some refuse even to call it the 'Holy Land', preferring instead the designation 'the Land of the Holy One'. In a weekly protest in Jerusalem against Israeli policies, Jewish radicals wear a T-shirt stating, 'There can be no holiness in an occupied city.' So, what is holiness: how do we recognize it? What *is* a holy place? What, indeed, is holy? These are crucial issues for all Christians, whether pilgrims to the Holy Land or those living as pilgrims at home. What is holy? Where, indeed, do we find God?

The root meaning of the Hebrew *qodesh*, the word usually trans- lated 'holy', is to separate, to set apart. It refers, first of all, to God as utterly Other, transcendent, with a vast gap between Creator and creature. But the divine touches and sanctifies earth. From the dawn of its history, Jerusalem as a Canaanite 'high place' becomes a sacred domain, locus of encounter with the gods, divine– human nexus. In the earliest reference in the Bible to 'Salem', the priest-king Melchizedek, perhaps around 2000 BC, blesses Abraham in the name of God Most High (Hebrew: *El Elyon*), bringing out bread and wine (Gen. 14.18). The idea of 'Holy Land' begins with Abraham and God's covenant with him – the dream of a 'prom- ised land': 'to your offspring I will give this land' (Gen. 12.7).

Later, after David has established Jerusalem as his religious and political capital, God himself comes to live on Mount Zion, in the biblical perspective. From the Holy of Holies, the innermost sanctuary in the Temple built by Solomon atop the Ophel Ridge in about 970 BC, the Ark of the Covenant radiates a circle of holiness: in later times, this circle was understood to consist of concentric zones of diminishing intensity, with the Court of Priests closest to the shrine, and outside this, the Court of Israelites and Women, and finally the Court of Gentiles. After the disappearance of the Ark, the Holy of Holies becomes a divine void, the primordial sacred space. The holy place is to be approached with awe, fear and trembling – only the purified priest can draw near. The 'Holiness Code' (Lev. 17—26) directs priest and people on the proper accession to the sanctuary, with its oft-repeated divine injunction: 'Be holy, for I am holy' (Lev. 11.44, 45; cf. 1 Peter 1.15, 16). The Psalms celebrate Zion and Jerusalem as 'the holy place': 'Who shall ascend the hill of the LORD? And who shall stand in his holy place? Those who have clean hands and pure hearts' (Ps. 24.3, 4a). Psalm 46 proclaims Jerusalem 'the city of God, the holy habitation of the Most High'. Even today, the pilgrim encounters a warning sign, erected by the Chief Rabbinate of Israel, at the last remnant of the Second Temple: 'You are approaching the holy site of the Western Wall, where the Divine Presence always rests.'

In Christianity the concept of the holy places developed after the Emperor Constantine's conversion in the fourth century AD and the visit of his mother Helena to this land to identify the holy places associated with the life, death and resurrection of Christ. Splendid Byzantine churches marked these places out as sites for worship and pilgrimage. Many became what the Celtic tradition calls 'thin places', where the veil between heaven and earth, between the human and divine, is easily crossed – where there is often, to this day, a palpable sense of God's presence, deepened by the prayers of the centuries. Here pilgrims sense what Rudolf Otto, in his classic work *The Idea of the Holy*, called 'the numinous'.

The example of Bethlehem

Every year thousands come to Bethlehem to visit the Basilica of the Nativity. A fortress of a church, built by Justinian in the sixth century on Constantinian foundations, it is an awesome place. The pilgrims enter by a low door, requiring them to bend in humility (though the original purpose of the door was merely to prevent people riding their horses in!), and find themselves in the mighty nave, with its stunning mosaics and soaring marble pillars. The church is built over the cave of the nativity, where a silver star marks the traditional birthplace of Christ. As if going into the depths of the earth, pilgrims descend steep steps to enter the grotto, where they get down on their knees to kiss the silver star placed upon the rock. It bears the Latin words '*Hic de Virgine Maria Jesus Christus natus est*'. That short word *hic* is found across the Holy Land, marking out holy places: it happened *here!*[1]

There is an unbroken tradition of prayer and pilgrimage at this site, where it is Christmas every day. The place of the nativity localizes the Incarnation, the Word made flesh who pitches his tent among us (John 1.14). It confronts us with the 'scandal of particularity' – for God to take on humanity for the sake of the whole world, there had to be one specific time and one concrete place where that happened. That place is Bethlehem, and here Christians ponder the wonder of God accepting human flesh and blood from Mary and, in Jesus, being born our brother. We would indeed bend low: the holy God was laid in the dirt and dust here in Bethlehem's stable . . . which is now the grotto of a magnificently adorned church, a site which pilgrims come to venerate each year.

But there is another side to Bethlehem and another answer to the questions, What is holy? Where can we find God? Where should we be looking for God? Where is God to be encountered today? Today, Bethlehem is a living Palestinian city, often noisy and congested, with honking buses and car horns blaring. Its concrete structures cling uneasily to the terraces; the cave of the nativity is at the top of a steep-sided mountain. Today, Bethlehem is hemmed in by the towering concrete Wall, Israel's Security Barrier, and is encircled by nine recently built Jewish settlements. While pilgrims and tourists may pass Bethlehem's military checkpoint at the Wall fairly freely, for Bethlehemites it is a humiliating ordeal to pass in or out, impossible without the right ID or special permits, issued only after complex form-filling and endless waiting. Many in Bethlehem are separated from their families and relatives in nearby Jerusalem. The statistics tell of increasing rates of emigration of Christians in recent years. In 1947 Bethlehem was 75 per cent Christian and 25 per cent Muslim. Today it is the other way around, for Christians are leaving in their droves, in search of a better life in the USA and elsewhere.[2]

A challenge from the gospel

Where do we find God? Where should we be looking for Christ? Is it possible for us to encounter him, not only in holy rocks and grottos but also in the broken lives of the oppressed? In Christ's parable:

> Then the king will say to those at his right hand, 'Come, you that are blessed by my Father, inherit the kingdom prepared for you from the foundation of the world; for I was hungry and you gave me food, I was thirsty and you gave me something to drink, I was a stranger and you welcomed me, I was naked and you gave me clothing, I was sick and you took care of me, I was in prison and you visited me . . . Truly I tell you, just as you did it to one of the least of these who are members of my family, you did it to me.'
>
> (Matt. 25.34–36, 40)

These words resonate strongly with the experience of the people of Bethlehem today. The local population of Bethlehem, both Christian and Muslim, have become prisoners in their own homes, living in the captivity of the occupied territories of the West Bank. A short distance from the Church of the Nativity, thousands are crammed into three major refugee camps.[3] Often stripped of their human dignity and human rights, high unemployment robs the camps' occupants of their residual self-worth. The Palestinians of Bethlehem have become strangers in their own land; the Wall has sliced mercilessly through their communities, meaning they are no longer able to access their ancestral olive groves or visit their relatives. They are sick in body, having problems in accessing the better healthcare facilities located in Jerusalem, and sick in the sense that they are weary, downcast, sick of soul, dispirited. Many remain hungry: the West Bank area consists mainly of highlands, with very little land suitable for growing arable crops – a meagre harvest is gleaned from the unproductive terraces of the barren mountains. And despair intensifies in the face of a faltering peace process.

The life of Jesus redefines holiness. The Incarnation redefines the holy. Now we touch the holy God in his incarnate life in Jesus. We see the holy, in Jesus, in the dirt of a Bethlehem stable, in the simplicity and poverty of Galilee, in the heartache and longing of his tears on the Mount of Olives, in the pain and isolation of Calvary, in the mystery of Easter – there, in these 'holy places', God's presence is to be discovered and welcomed. This Jesus invites us to find him in 'these brothers and sisters of mine' who are hungry, broken, stripped, imprisoned, estranged. The Incarnation overturns the traditional dichotomy between sacred and secular, between 'holy' and 'unholy'. It challenges us to glimpse the divine in the dust, and to be alert to God's presence in the broken.[4] It alerts us to the possibility that Christ might be close at hand, incognito, waiting to be recognized and greeted.

In Christ's parable the question is: 'Lord, when did we *see* you . . . ?' As pilgrims on earth, we need to open our eyes! Often in the Gospels seeing is a metaphor for believing. To downcast disciples Jesus says: 'Look around you, and see how the fields are ripe for harvesting' (John 4.35). On Easter day 'their eyes were kept from recognizing him' until the eucharistic moment of discovery: 'Then their eyes were opened, and they recognized him' (Luke 24.16, 31). The question is: Where do we see Jesus today, and where do we miss him? Our prayer might echo that of Bartimaeus: 'My teacher, let me see again' (Mark 10.51). In Bethlehem, what can you see, beyond the churches and olive-wood shops? We have a choice: we can walk with blinkered eyes, vision narrowed by routine or personal urgencies; with shut eyes, closed by prejudice; with lazy eyes, inattentive. Or we can walk with open eyes, ready to glimpse God, in holy places and beyond.

Sacramental land?

Bethlehem has always been a sacramental place, where God reveals himself in outward and visible signs. In a powerfully sacramental action, Boaz covers the sleeping Ruth with his blanket, a symbol of the radical acceptance of an outsider (Ruth 3.9). Her grandson David, the shepherd boy, is anointed with the oil that Samuel pours over his head, and the divine Spirit comes upon him, sealing his call to the kingship (1 Sam. 16.13). Jesus, son of David, born in Bethlehem, is recognized as the revelation of God in tangible human flesh and blood, the very sacrament of God:

> We declare to you what was from the beginning, what we have heard, what we have seen with our eyes, what we have looked at and touched with our hands, concerning the word of life – this life was revealed, and we have seen it and testify to it. (1 John 1.1–2a)

The very name 'Bethlehem' means, in Hebrew, 'House of Bread'. The highlight of every pilgrim's visit is the celebration of the Eucharist. But this should alert us to the sacrament of Bethlehem we see at every turn: God waiting to greet us in the poor. The recognition of the presence of Jesus in torn bread and poured-out wine calls us to look for him in the broken lives and crushed grapes of the bruised and wounded in Bethlehem today. They become an outward and visible sign of God's presence. Mother Teresa of Calcutta challenges us: 'If you really love Jesus in the Eucharist, you will naturally want to put that love into action by serving him in his distressing disguise of the poorest of the poor. We cannot separate these two things: the Eucharist and the Poor.'[5] John Chrysostom, in the fourth century, argued:

> Do you wish to honour the body of Christ? Do not ignore him when he is naked. Do not pay him homage in the temple clad in silk, only then to neglect him outside where he is cold and ill-clad. He who said: 'This is my body' is the same who said: 'You saw me hungry and you gave me no food', and 'whatever you did to the least of my brothers you

did also to me . . .' What good is it if the Eucharistic table is over loaded with golden chalices when your brother is dying of hunger? Start by satisfying his hunger and then with what is left you may adorn the altar as well.[6]

In this connection, perhaps we should be more alert to the heresy, or mixed messages, of the carols we sing each Christmas. We express our theology in hymns but sometimes it can be skewed, driving deeper into us unhelpful ideas as we sing so sweetly. In 'O Little Town of Bethlehem' we sing, 'O holy Child of Bethlehem, descend to us we pray', but the point of the story is that God is here, below, in the dust of the stable, not in a sterile faraway heaven, needing to be dragged back down to earth. We sing, 'Where meek souls will receive him, still the dear Christ enters in' but in these words lies the danger of excessively spiritualizing an event which proclaims that God is with us in human flesh and blood. He is here in human lives, not only in pious souls! In the carol 'Away in a Manger' the error is compounded: 'I love thee, Lord Jesus! Look down from the sky.' Perhaps we should be looking down, not up: down to those in the gutter, those who are marginalized and cast out . . .

There is still a role for holy places in the traditional sense, but only if they do not become idols, things to be venerated in themselves. The holy places can be powerful reminders of the God who comes to us, markers in the soil of where God has walked. Yes, they can be 'sacred spaces' where we may encounter the Divine. But they need to be seen as clues to the type of God we believe in – a passionate and compassionate God who enters fully into our human condition and is close to the brokenhearted. The rocks and churches of the 'holy places' testify to a God who empties himself, a dusty and dirty God who involves himself fully in the pain of humanity.

John of Damascus in the eighth century called the holy places 'receptacles of divine energy'. Maybe we can think of them not so much as 'receptacles' but as places of divine energy in the sense that they can disturb us, challenge us, question us. They can stimulate and inspire us in our search for God. They are not ends in themselves but potentially helps on the journey: *signposts* to where Christ may be revealing himself today in human lives.

The Jewish idea of *tikkun*, often translated as 'repairing the world', can help alert us to the presence of God in unlikely places. The sixteenth-century kabbalist Isaac Luria taught that in the mystery of creation, God poured his divine light into vessels over the world. These could not contain the effulgence of God's presence and shattered into many fragments, trapping sparks of the divine light amid their shards as they fell to earth. It is the vocation of humanity, taught Luria, to release and unlock these holy sparks amid the world's brokenness and return them to God through prayer and service. We are to discover the hidden presences of God in the midst of the world's mire. We must discern opportunities for 'gathering the sparks' – taking small steps to release the trapped glimmers of light that lie half buried in the dust of the world's confusions.

Three things can inspire us about this vision of God's holiness. First, elements of divine light glint all around us, if only we open our eyes and look beneath the surface. Second, God asks us to work with him as partners in a divine–human synergy whereby the fragmentedness of the world may be healed. Third, little actions, tiny steps of reconciliation, matter very much and contribute to the restoration of wholeness bit by bit. Do not despise the humble moments or small actions: they help gather up a fragmented spark or two and return them to God. They help 'repair the world'.[7]

God waits to reveal himself in surprising locations and in surprising people. Theophany, divine disclosure, breaks out unsummoned. That, perhaps, is the message of Bethlehem. And the question of Bethlehem is for every time and place: What is holy? Where is God?

Questions for reflection

1 Where do you find God? Where are you most aware of his presence?
2 What 'holy places' exist in your life? Where have you discovered 'thin places'?

3 How difficult do you find it to encounter God in the sick, broken and homeless? What might help you to do this?
4 How do you find yourself responding in a 'holy place'?
5 Is the 'Holy Land' an appropriate designation for Israel/Palestine? Why?

For further reading

M. Prior and W. Taylor (eds), *Christians in the Holy Land* (Buckhurst Hill: Scorpion Publishing, 1994)

M. Raheb, *Bethlehem Besieged: Stories of Hope in Times of Trouble* (Minneapolis: Augsburg Fortress, 2004)

D. Tsimhoni, *Christian Communities in Jerusalem and the West Bank Since 1948: An Historical, Social and Political Study* (Westport, CT and London: Praeger, 1993)

P. W. L. Walker and G. Tomlin, *Walking in His Steps* (Oxford: Lion, 2003)

P. W. L. Walker, *Holy City, Holy Places?* (Oxford: Clarendon Press, 1990)

Figure 3 Waters of identity: the Jordan at Yardinet

3

The river's questions

Who am I?

————•◆•————

The River Jordan gets its name from the Hebrew *Yarden*, meaning 'to descend'. It begins its life in the springs of Banias, at the
foothills of Mount Hermon. It cascades through the verdant
Galilean hills, eroding its way to the Sea of Galilee. Because only
limited amounts of precious water are allowed to flow from the
reservoir of the Sea of Galilee down to the Dead Sea, south of
the lake the Jordan becomes more of a stream, flowing in a hidden
channel cut into the valley floor, which is bounded to east
and west by the precipitous limestone escarpment of the great
African–Syrian rift.

Today this southern section of the River Jordan is a determinant
of identity both for the Jew and the Arab. For the Arab it marks
the edge of a hoped-for Palestinian state developing on the
West Bank of the river (and beside the sea at Gaza). For the Jew
it marks the edge of *Eretz Israel*, and the limit of land conquered
in the 1967 war. From ancient times the Jordan acquired crucial
symbolic significance, for it was here that the Exodus journey
from slavery in Egypt neared its completion. The Hebrews
advanced across the river into the land, the waters separating
as the priests bore the Ark of the Covenant, symbol of God's
pilgrim presence with his people. This was a moment of profound
self-definition – the Hebrews were slaves no longer, they were
becoming 'Israelites' as they entered the land of promise at the
Jordan (Josh. 3). As Psalm 114 celebrates it: 'When Israel went out
from Egypt . . . The sea looked and fled; Jordan turned back.'

In the New Testament the same River Jordan becomes a place
where identity is discovered and affirmed. It is at the Jordan that

John the Baptist, issuing his radical call to repentance and baptism, is questioned by a delegation of priests and Levites sent from Jerusalem. They want to discover his status and his role and their question is emphatically repeated, in the fourth Gospel, three times: 'Who are you?'; 'What do you say about yourself?' (John 1.19, 22). The Jews framed their question with a certain set of expectations: Are you the Messiah? Elijah? The prophet? They looked at the question of identity through a lens and mindset shaped by messianic expectations.

On his part, John's own self-definition is drawn from Isaiah 40: 'I am the voice of one crying out in the wilderness, "Make straight the way of the Lord".' For John, the Jordan becomes a place of self-discovery as he leaves his previous life (perhaps among the Essenes at nearby Qumran) and clarifies his vocation as precursor of the Saviour. John defines himself by his lifestyle and his way of dressing – for he attires himself, according to Mark, in the self-same way as did Elijah the prophet (Mark 1.6; cf. 2 Kings 1.8). His very clothes make a powerful statement about his self-identity. As Jesus comes to the Jordan for baptism, he experiences a moment of great affirmation: his identity is clarified and proclaimed, as we shall consider below.

Identity in the Holy Land today

One of the most complex and baffling issues facing the visitor to the Holy Land concerns identity. Who am I? What defines me? What are the determinants of identity? As Bernard Lewis reminds us in the title of his book *The Multiple Identities of the Middle East*, the building of a sense of identity is multi-layered. Factors which shape it include origins/birthplace, language, religion, blood/race and, we might add in the West, sexuality. Events in history also contribute massively to the development of identity: for the Jew the horrors of the Holocaust, for the Palestinian the event called the *Nakba*, the Disaster – the loss of ancestral lands in the 1948 conflict which the Israelis celebrate as the War of Independence. The forging of identity involves questions of loyalty and belonging, of self-awareness and self-perception. It is also worked out collectively in relation to the Other, to those who are 'not us' – what makes *me* different from *you*?

Jewish identity

What *is* a Jew? The Law of Return, established after the creation of the State of Israel in 1948, gives any Jew the right to settle in Israel. As a political power Israel seeks to develop itself as a 'Jewish State'. Some have questioned whether this amounts to a racist state. The Law of Return itself fails to define who is a Jew and the question of what constitutes Jewish identity remains a matter of some controversy. Halakah (rabbinic tradition) gives two possible answers.

First, one can be a Jew by birth. Jewishness is a racial or ethnic issue, a matter of Jewish blood – one must be born of a Jewish mother (cf. Lev. 24.10; Deut. 7.1–5). Reform and Liberal Judaism accept as Jewish the child of either a Jewish father or mother, as long as the child receives a Jewish, religious upbringing. Orthodox Judaism generally accepts as Jewish a person born of a Jewish mother, even if that person forsakes his or her faith or converts to another religion. That is, a birth-Jew who leaves Judaism is still a Jew as it is a matter of ethnicity, even if he or she lives an atheistic or secular lifestyle.[1] The issue of blood-lines is complex, but research in 2000 by Michael Hammers of Arizona University, among others, has established that genetically Jews and Arabs are virtually identical, sharing from ancient days the heritage of a common Y chromosome.

Second, one can be Jewish by belief. If a Gentile completes the conversion process, accepting Jewish faith and religious practice – which includes circumcision for males – he or she can become Jewish. Orthodox Judaism is however very strict in its requirements and has cast doubt on the validity of the conversion process and ceremony in some liberal traditions.

In Jerusalem, Jewish identity reflects the cultures of the Diaspora (scattering across the globe), including a diversity of communities that originated in many different parts of the world. There are three main groupings: Askenazi Jews, who are of German or Eastern European descent (making up 80 per cent of all Jews worldwide); Sephardic Jews, originating from the Iberian Peninsula; and Mizrahim Jews or Orientals, including those from eastern countries and also from north Africa.

Because of its distinctive attire, the most visible community is the Haredi or Ultra Orthodox, some of whom are Hasidic, belonging to the revivalist and devotional traditions that originated with Israel ben Eliezer (1700–60). The men identify themselves by their beards and side locks (*peyos*, see Lev. 19.27), their black jackets (*reckel*), and the long fringes or tassels (*tzitzit*) which descend from a vest (*tallit katan*) in order to remind them of the 613 commandments (see Num. 15.39). They will also wear on their forehead the phylactery or *tefillin*, a small box containing words from the Torah, with its leather straps going up the arm (in fulfilment of Deut. 6.8). The men wear a black felt hat (*fedora*) or a fur hat (*shtreimel*); like all religious Jews they wear a skullcap or *kippah*. The women cover their hair with a scarf or a wig as it is not to be seen in public. Of course Orthodox Jews also identify themselves by their strict observance of the Sabbath and of kosher dietary laws. Mainly Askenazi Jews, although 20 per cent are Sephardic, the Ultra Orthodox in Jerusalem often live in tightly knit, closed communities which resemble the ghettos of Eastern Europe. This way of living preserves a strong sense of origins and of separateness, perhaps also revealing a mistrust of others in the wake of the Holocaust.

Palestinian identity

The word 'Palestine' was first used by Hadrian in the second century when – Latinizing the Greek word for Philistine – he called Judaea 'Palestina'. The designation Palestine was not used officially until the time of the British Mandate after the First World War, when it became the title for the land. The concept of Palestine is therefore relatively recent. Indeed, as Rashid Khalidi argues in his book *Palestinian Identity: The Constitution of a Modern Consciousness*, Palestinian Arab national identity developed in relation to the Other, that is, political Zionism. During the four hundred years of the Ottoman period the country was the Province of Syria; the Turks discouraged particularism and wanted to foster a widespread Ottoman identity and loyalty among the empire's subjects.

The issue of Palestinian identity is bound up with the vexed question of citizenship and nationality. One very painful symbol of this remains the identity card, which must be carried by all Palestinians and shown at the nearly four hundred checkpoints on the West Bank. Frequently one sees the sign 'Slow! Barrier ahead! Prepare to present documents!' This is a bitter experience of often daily humiliation for Palestinians who need to traverse the checkpoints in order to go to work or see family. The 'proof of identity', the issuing of which is almost totally under Israeli control, comes in one of two forms. The Blue ID card is issued to those who live within the 1948 borders of the State of Israel or in Jerusalem: these include Israeli Arabs who may have Israeli passports. The Green Card is for Palestinians who live in the West Bank and Gaza; some may possess Jordanian passports (but cannot live in Jordan). Large numbers of Palestinian Jerusalemites have been stripped of their residency rights in recent years, their treasured Blue ID cards confiscated.[2]

Palestinian identity is revealed in traditional dress. Muslim women attire themselves in a loose-fitting robe called the *thob*, often in black or a dark colour, bearing a square embroidered panel (*qabbeh*) on the front: this reveals the identity of the wearer, for each village has its own unique designs. Over this a long coat (*jillayeh*) may be worn. Hair will be covered with a *hijjab* or headscarf, in accordance with the Qur'an's requirement to dress modestly. Traditional Muslim men may wear a *thob*, a long white shirt-like garment, and the *keffiyah* headdress, which became a symbol of Palestinian national resistance in the 1936–9 Arab revolt. Black patterns on white are specifically Palestinian, while the red-on-white version is Jordanian.

Christian identity

Local Christians, are of course, Palestinian; there is a small community of Jewish Christians, also known as Messianic Jews. Indigenous Palestinian Christian men and women often stand out because they wear conservative western-style attire. In Jerusalem, Christians are known for their schools, hospitals, church bells and crosses, pork and alcohol! The bewildering range of Christian communities, encompassing a diversity of ethnicities, crystallizes into four major groupings. First, the Orthodox Church comprises mainly Palestinians and Greeks; there are also notable Russian and Romanian communities. Second, the Oriental Orthodox churches, developing their understanding of Christ in terms of his 'one nature', are thus sometimes called Monophysites: these include the Armenian, Coptic, Ethiopian and Syrian Christians. Their presence in the land dates from the fourth century, when they arrived as pilgrims and built monasteries and hospices. Third, members of the Roman Catholic Church are known locally as 'the Latins'; they originated here at the time of the Crusades. In addition to local Palestinian members, these embrace a range of different nationalities and religious orders. Also in the Latin fold are parts of the Orthodox family that united with Rome in the eighteenth century: these 'uniate' churches include the Greek Catholics, which form the largest Christian community in the country. Fourth, there are the Reformed Christians, who arrived in the nineteenth century in connection with European interests in the Holy Land: these include the Anglicans and Lutherans.

The identity of these different communities is bound up with their unique histories and revealed in language and outward dress. The Franciscans are noticeable in their brown habits, while the French 'White Fathers' get their name from the colour of their cassocks. It has been said of the clergy of the different traditions that 'by their hats you shall know them' – the Armenian priests with the black-pointed hood that reminds them of the peak of beloved Mount Ararat; the Greek Orthodox with their stove-pipe caps; the Syriac priests bearing a dark head-covering sparkling with 13 crosses – one for each of the apostles and one for the Lord.

Jesus at the Jordan

As he emerges, dripping, from the waters of the Jordan, Jesus receives a triple attestation: the voice, the Spirit and the rending of heaven. The Spirit comes to empower him for his ministry ahead; the divine voice declares to him: 'You are my Son, the Beloved.' As the evangelists tell the story, there is a clear echo here not only of Psalm 2 but also of the Servant Song of Isaiah 42. Indeed, as Oscar Cullmann maintains, this servant image is a key to Jesus' self-identity and 'opens for us, most clearly, the secret of his self-consciousness'.[3] The tearing or ripping apart of heaven speaks of the possibility of heaven and earth now being reunited in the life-work of Jesus: heaven is closed up no longer.

It is at the headwaters of the Jordan, at Caesarea Philippi (Banias), that Jesus himself raises the issue of his identity with his double question: 'Who do people say I am? Who do you say I am?' Once again various differing expectations are placed on Jesus. Can he be Elijah or Jeremiah come back to life, one of the prophets? Jesus seems to reject Peter's greeting of him as Messiah, a title which carried hopes that its bearer would be a political liberator who would overthrow the Roman yoke. Rather he describes himself in terms of a 'Son of Man' who is destined to die and rise again (Mark 8.31). Here, at the river, we gain an insight into Jesus' own sense of destiny, vocation and identity. For the Christian, too, our identity lies deep in the Jordan, for it is in the waters of baptism that we get the clearest indicators of both our destiny and our dignity.

Christian identity is defined by the Incarnation

As Jesus received at the Jordan the profound affirmation, 'You are my beloved Son', so in the waters of baptism we are reborn as God's children. God delights in us: 'You are my beloved daughter!' 'You are my cherished son!' Jesus comes to lead us into a relationship with God, one in which we can enter his intimacy with God as we make our own his prayer, 'Abba! Father!'

Paul tells us: 'When we cry, "Abba! Father!" it is that very Spirit bearing witness with our spirit that we are children of God' (Rom. 8.15, 16). As John puts it: 'See what love the Father has given us, that we should be called children of God; *and that is what we are*' (1 John 3.1, emphasis added). The Letter to the Hebrews tells us that Jesus shares not only our flesh and blood but also our human suffering: 'For this reason Jesus is not ashamed to call them brothers and sisters' (Heb. 2.11). Our identity and worth do not come from what other people say about us. They come from what God says about us and, in baptism, God declares that we are his beloved.

Christian identity is defined by the cross and resurrection

Augustine says: 'We are an Easter People and Alleluia is our song!' As Christ's descent into the waters of the Jordan and his emergence foreshadow his death and resurrection, so baptism affirms that our identity is essentially paschal in character. For Christians, the waters of baptism are a place of death and resurrection effecting a dying to self, asphyxiating the old way of life. Our rising from the water unites us to Christ's resurrection. This is the Christian 'passover', the passing from death to new life.

We must live the mystery. Baptism is not a 'once upon a time' matter but a reality which shapes our lives each day with its truth and power. On the cross our old nature was crucified and in the waters it was drowned. Paul tells us: 'You also must consider yourselves dead to sin and alive to God in Christ Jesus' (Rom. 6.11). The key words, in the present tense, are 'consider yourselves', 'reckon yourselves'. *Look at yourselves again. Remember who you really are in Christ.* The biblical scholar John Ziesler comments that Paul is talking about the basic 'self-understanding' of the Christian.[4] In Christ we are dead, finished with sin, unresponsive to it; we are potentially alert to God. So become what you are. Celebrate and live out your new identity in Christ, your potential and your calling. Remind yourself of your new dignity. Become self-aware and stay awake. At every moment when sin tries to raise its ugly head, be decisive: 'Do not let sin exercise dominion in your mortal bodies . . . present yourselves to God as those who have been brought from death to life' (Rom. 6.12, 13). We need to renew our baptismal dedication to God daily and offer ourselves afresh to God. As Paul puts it: 'I have been crucified with Christ; and it is no longer I who live, but it is Christ who lives in me' (Gal. 2.19, 20).

Powerfully, the Jordan waters summon us to drench ourselves in the realities signified by baptism: this dying to sin and selfishness, and rising to newness of life. Each day God calls us to enter more fully into the Easter mystery, to appropriate it and make it ever more deeply our own. God invites us to take the plunge, to wade into the waters and to meet him face to face: it is here that liberation and re-creation will be experienced. We have to return to the waters, as we do in worship each Easter. We have to reclaim the victory of baptism.

Christian identity is defined by the gift of the Spirit

As at his baptism Jesus saw the Spirit descend on him as a dove, so the Holy Spirit constitutes the Christian and is the key to Christian identity. Literally: for 'Christian' means follower of the *Christos*, the anointed one. In Luke's perspective, the words that Jesus quotes soon after his baptism find an echo in Christian experience:

> The Spirit of the Lord is upon me,
> because he has anointed me
> to bring good news to the poor.
> He has sent me to proclaim release to the captives
> and recovery of sight to the blind,
> to let the oppressed go free.   (Luke 4.18)

The Spirit is given to equip us for a ministry of courage and compassion, a ministry that reaches out untiringly to the broken and captive. The liberating Spirit, like dynamite, energizes the Church: 'You will receive power [*dunamis*] when the Holy Spirit has come upon you; and you will be my witnesses' (Acts 1.8). As the baptismal prayer puts it: 'May God, who has received you by baptism into his Church, pour upon you the riches of his grace, that within the company of Christ's pilgrim people you may daily be renewed by his anointing Spirit, and come to the inheritance of the saints in glory. Amen.'[5]

Paul offers us a radically inclusive vision for the baptized:

> In Christ Jesus you are all children of God through faith. As many of you as were baptized into Christ have clothed yourselves with Christ. There is no longer Jew

or Greek, there is no longer slave or free, there is no longer male and female; for all of you are one in Christ Jesus.

(Gal. 3.26–28)

He declares: 'And if you belong to Christ, then you are Abraham's offspring, heirs according to the promise' (3.29). Interpreted more widely, these words hold out to us a vision for all the Children of Abraham – Jew, Christian and Muslim – our identity springing from God, and our radical equality before him.

Questions for reflection

1 How far does your faith define or determine your own sense of identity? In Jerusalem, religious identity is manifested in dress: how prepared are you to reveal your religious affiliation outwardly in some way?
2 How would you describe yourself to someone you are meeting for the first time?
3 How can you live more deeply your baptismal identity?
4 When different identities are sharply defined, does this make it easier or more difficult to relate to the Other?
5 What threatens our sense of identity today? What affirms us? How can we encourage each other?

For further reading

J. Entine, *Abraham's Children: Race, Identity and the DNA of the Chosen People* (New York: Grand Central Publishing, 2007)

W. K. Kawar, *Threads of Identity: Preserving Palestinian Costume and Heritage* (Nicosia, Cyprus: Rimal Publications, 2010)

R. Khalidi, *Palestinian Identity: The Constitution of a Modern Consciousness* (New York: Columbia University Press, 1998)

B. Lewis, *The Multiple Identities of the Middle East* (New York: Schocken, 2001)

Figure 4 Out of the depths: monastic cave of Khallat ed-Danabiya opens onto Wadi Makkuk

4

The cave's questions

How can I face the darkness?

———•◆•———

One of the things that strikes pilgrims to the Holy Land is the frequency with which they are required to go down into caves! Many of the holy places are, in fact, caves. The pilgrim descends underground into sacred grottos and caverns, and, in the subterranean mystery, finds God. These hidden chambers in the bowels of the earth turn out to be liminal places, thresholds of the divine.

There are awesome caves associated with the Old Testament. The first to be mentioned in the Bible (Gen. 23) is the Cave of Mecpelah, the burial place of Abraham and Sarah; today, this is below the great Herodian building at Hebron, which can be entered either at the Muslim side as a mosque or at the Jewish side as an adjoining synagogue. Sinai preserves the memory of Moses in the cave; to him God says: 'While my glory passes by I will put you in a cleft of the rock' (Exod. 33.22). At Sinai we recall how Elijah fled and hid in a cave on Horeb when he was in a state of fear and stress. Here God questions him: 'What are you doing here, Elijah?' (1 Kings 19.9, 13). There is also the Cave of Elijah at the foot of Mount Carmel. The Cave of Zedekiah near the Damascus Gate in Jerusalem is the largest man-made cave in the land, extending 230 metres under the Old City, and served as a quarry for Herod's rebuilding of the Second Temple. The mysterious caves of Qumran, in marl canyons overlooking the Dead Sea, held for almost two thousand years the precious documents of the Essenes, rediscovered in 1947. In the Islamic tradition, a mysterious cave below the great stony outcrop sheltered by the Dome of the Rock in Jerusalem is known as 'the well of souls', while we recall that it was after three years' solitude in the Cave of Hira near Mecca that Muhammad received the revelations of the Qur'an.

There are caves bound up with the New Testament story. The traditional birthplace of John the Baptist is found in the cave of Ein Karem, while the domestic cave of Mary's House in Nazareth is now preserved under the largest church in the Middle East, the Basilica of the Annunciation. Around the Mount of Olives there are caves preserving special memories: the cave of Eleona where Constantine built a basilica to celebrate the teaching of Jesus, known today as the Paternoster site; the grotto at the foot of the Mount of Olives in Gethsemane which scholars believe was the place of the arrest of Jesus.[1] Nearby, one descends over eighty steps from the Kidron valley to the Tomb of Mary, a cavernous underground church which contains her empty sepulchre.

At Bethlehem, as we recall, the focal point of devotion and pilgrimage is the cave of the nativity under Justinian's sixth-century basilica. The religious imagination, fed by images from Christmas cards or nativity plays, expects to find a wooden-roofed stable in Bethlehem; the pilgrim instead encounters a mysterious cave deep in the earth. As Justin Martyr wrote in AD 160 in his *Dialogue with Trypho the Jew*: 'When the Child was born in Bethlehem, because there was nowhere to rest in that place, Joseph went into a cave very close to the village.' Origen, writing in 248, testifies: 'In Bethlehem you are shown the cave where he was born . . . Even those who do not share our faith recognize that the Jesus whom Christians adore was born in this cave' (*Contra Celsus* 1.51).

The most important cave for Christians is the cave of Christ's burial and resurrection, parts of which are preserved in the *edicule* or 'little house' in the Church of the Resurrection, known as the Holy Sepulchre.[2] Eusebius of Caesarea, the fourth-century church historian, describes with great joy in his *Life of Constantine* how the cave of the resurrection was rediscovered beneath the earth in 326, after it had been deliberately covered over in 135 by Hadrian's pagan temple, built in an attempt to stamp out early devotion to the site: 'As layer after layer of the subsoil came into view, the venerable and most holy memorial of the Saviour's resurrection, beyond all our hopes, came into view: the holy of holies, the Cave, was like our Saviour, restored to life.'

In the Bible, caves represent negative human experiences. First, caves are places of death – as Abraham seeks a cave into which to lay his dead wife. They are tombs, graves, scenes of sadness and grief. At the tomb of Lazarus, which John tells us was a cave, Jesus was 'again greatly disturbed' (John 11.38). In the Hebrew Scriptures the cave often recalls the Pit of Sheol, the world of the dead, the underworld, the abyss. Josephus gloomily states: 'Hades is a subterranean place, wherein the light of this world does not shine . . . there must be in it perpetual darkness' (*Discourse to the Greeks concerning Hades* 1). The Pit represented death and fear, Psalm 30.9 asking: 'What profit is there in my death, if I go down to the Pit? Will the dust praise you? Will it tell of your faithfulness?'

Second, they are places of refuge and fear, bolt-holes for retreat from danger. 'The hand of Midian prevailed over Israel; and because of Midian the Israelites provided for themselves hiding-places in the mountains, caves and strongholds' (Judg. 6.2; see also Isa. 2.21). Obadiah concealed the prophets in caves to escape Jezebel's sword (1 Kings 18.4). Desperate lamentations and cries for help echo from the depths. Psalm 142, called 'A Maskil of David. When he was in the cave', relates to his escape to the cave of Adullam (1 Sam. 22.1). 'With my voice I cry to the Lord . . . Bring me out of prison' (Ps. 142.1, 7). Psalm 57 is likewise attributed to David, 'when he fled from Saul, in the cave': 'In the shadow of your wings I will take refuge, until the destroying storms pass by' (Ps. 57.1).

Jesus himself often passed such caverns of fear. Towering over the valley path from Capernaum to Nazareth and overlooking the north-western corner of the Sea of Galilee near Magdala, the dramatic Arbel cliffs are honeycombed by four hundred caves. In 37 BC Galilean zealots barricaded themselves here, as Josephus tells us: 'lurking in caves . . . opening up onto mountain precipices that were inaccessible from any quarter, except by some tortuous and extremely narrow paths . . . the cliff in front of them dropped sheer down' (*Jewish War*, 305, 310). The forces of Herod the Great reached the fugitive rebels by lowering cages down from the top: soldiers with flaming spears smoked them out to their death.

Early Christian writers began to glimpse the symbolism of the caves. Eusebius of Caesarea notices a triad of 'mystic caves' which testify to three cardinal points of the then newly written Creed of Nicaea: 'He was incarnate ... He was crucified ... He ascended.'

> In the same region, Constantine recovered three sites revered for three mystical caves and enhanced them with opulent structures. On the cave of the first theophany [Bethlehem] he conferred appropriate marks of honour; at the one where the ultimate Ascension occurred [the Mount of Olives] he consecrated a memorial on the mountain ridge; between these, at the scene of the great struggle [Calvary and the tomb of Christ], [he raised] the sign of salvation and victory.[3]

What, then, is the meaning of the caves in the sacred landscape of the Holy Land? What questions do they pose to us in our life-pilgrimage? We shall now explore three ways in which God works in the subterranean gloom, and identify four spiritualities which spring up from the depths.

God enters the depths

The caves declare that God reaches down to the deepest human need. There is no dark corner, no recess of grief, no hidden fear, no gloom of bereavement, no abyss of despair, no emptiness, no depths of misery that God cannot enter and transform. The God of the New Testament is a descending God. As Paul celebrates in his letter to the Philippians, Jesus humbles himself and empties himself to be found in human form (Phil. 2). This is the message of the cave of the nativity. It is precisely *there, in the depths of human need*, that he begins his redeeming work. In the Incarnation, the divine Creator Word enters the very depth of creation. The Western antiphon for Christmas Eve celebrates the kenosis or self-emptying of God's Word: 'For while all things were in quiet silence, and the night was in the midst of her course, Thy almighty Word leapt down from heaven from thy royal throne' (cf. Wisd. 18.14, 15).

In his Passion, Christ penetrates the lowest parts of the earth, the underworld. He enters the captivities of human fear and despair, the most profound anxieties of humanity. This is experienced very poignantly by pilgrims at the cave known as the 'sacred pit' deep below the Church of St Peter Gallicantu on Mount Zion, which marks the traditional site of the house of Caiaphas. The Herodian cave cut deep in the rock is identified as the prison into which Jesus was thrown while waiting for Caiaphas to assemble his fellow-accusers on the night of the Passion. Deep and claustrophobic, it evokes the Psalm's cry: 'Out of the depths I cry to you, O LORD. Lord, hear my voice!' (Ps. 130.1, 2). Another Psalm, which Christians recall after each Good Friday, conveys the desperation of this incarceration:

> I am counted among those who go down to the Pit;
> I am like those who have no help,
> like those forsaken among the dead . . .
> like those whom you remember no more . . .
> I am shut in so that I cannot escape;
> my eye grows dim through sorrow.
>
> (Ps. 88.4, 5, 8, 9)

But God not only enters the depths, he also transforms them: the cave becomes the place of salvation.

God works in the darkness

The Apostles' Creed tells us: 'He descended into hell.' Jesus is buried in the depths of the earth, but in the mystery of Holy Saturday the work of redemption is being accomplished silently, secretly, in the darkness of the grave. Christ is busy in the underworld: 'Christ . . . was put to death in the flesh, but made alive in the spirit, in which also he went and made a proclamation to the spirits in prison' (1 Pet. 3.18, 19). An Orthodox hymn sings the liberating truth:

41

> You descended to earth's depths,
> And smashed the eternal bars
> Which held the captives fast.[4]

An Easter day hymn exults: 'Today the Master despoiled Hades and raised them that from ages past were in fetters and held in grievous bondage.'[5] The prison of the cave-tomb becomes the starting point for humanity's journey to freedom.

God acts mysteriously

The mystic caves represent, too, the mysterious workings of God, his hidden purposes, often unfathomable and unsearchable: 'We speak God's wisdom, secret and hidden ... the Spirit searches everything, even the depths of God' (1 Cor. 2.7, 10). The darkness of the cave speaks to us of the mystery of God. God is always beyond our best concepts and categories, and human language cannot communicate his wonder. We can move beyond words to the prayer of dumbfounded amazement. This is the apophatic tradition, the *via negativa*: we come to the point where we admit the limits of our language when attempting to speak of God. The question posed to Job confronts us too: 'Can you find out the deep things of God? Can you find out the limit of the Almighty? ... Deeper than Sheol – what can you know?' (Job 11.7, 8). Isaiah confesses: 'Truly, you are a God who hides himself' (Isa. 45.15). With Paul we say: 'O the depth of the riches and wisdom and knowledge of God! How unsearchable are his judgements and how inscrutable his ways!' (Rom. 11.33).

A spirituality of descent

In the history of Christian spirituality the metaphor of ascent prevails: the image of going up to God. The way to God seems to be up, up, up. Influenced by Platonic ideas in the fourth century, Gregory of Nyssa uses the climbing of mountains as a model of Christian perfection in his *Life of Moses*. Writing at the monastery at Mount Sinai, the abbot John Climacus (579–649) suggests that the virtues form 30 rungs on the *Ladder of Divine Ascent*. St Bonaventure writes in his work *The Journey of the Mind into God* of the 'mind's ascent to God'. Even John of the Cross, in his masterpiece *The Ascent of Mount Carmel*, uses this model of going up to God and leaving worldly things behind.[6]

Ascent resonates with the modern desire for self-advancement and the seeking of promotion, 'going up the ladder', acquiring ever greater power and status. It suggests that one must renounce the world and get away from it in order to find God. But as N. Gordon Cosby writes of the descending God: 'If God is going down and we are going up, it is obvious that we are going in different directions . . . We will be evading God and missing the whole purpose of our existence.'[7] Paul Tillich, in his groundbreaking study *The Shaking of the Foundations*, invites us to rediscover the metaphor of the depths of God:

> Most of our life continues on the surface. We are enslaved by the routine of our daily lives . . . We are in constant motion and never stop to plunge into the depth. We talk and talk and never listen to the voices speaking to our depth and from our depth . . . It is comfortable to live on the surface . . . It is painful to break away from it and to descend into an unknown ground.[8]

We are summoned to quit superficial living and risk a descent into the depths, where we may find God and in the process, rediscover ourselves. As Richard Foster put it: 'Superficiality is the curse of our age . . . The desperate need today is not for a greater number of intelligent people, or gifted people, but for deep people.'[9]

A spirituality of darkness

In the Christian mystical tradition, we encounter God powerfully in the darkness. For John of the Cross, in the sixteenth century, the place of darkness, the 'dark night', becomes a place of transformation:

O Guiding Night!
O night more lovely than dawn!
O night that united
the Lover with his beloved,
transforming the beloved in her Lover![10]

The Spanish mystic sees the 'dark night of the soul' as a place of potential blessing. John gives three reasons for using this image of darkness to describe the encounter with God in prayer. First, in the dark we cannot actually see. Our five senses normally hold us captive in a state of attachment to the material world, and sometimes get us stuck to material things, so there are times when we need to pray with our eyes closed – in the darkness. Second, in the dark we can't make out obstacles or turnings along the path, or sense the way clearly. So in prayer we must be prepared to venture into undiscovered, unfamiliar terrain, along pathways we have yet to tread. Third, the darkness can also represent the times we think we cannot pray, when we can't find the words, when we don't feel anything towards God, perhaps when we are spiritually confused. John assures us that abiding in the darkness of God can be authentic prayer. In the darkness we can make the greatest discoveries of God. John's poems echo the ancient hymn of Easter praise, the *Exultet*: 'This is the night when Jesus Christ broke the chains of death and rose triumphant from the grave! The power of this night dispels all evil, washes guilt away, restores lost innocence, brings mourners joy!' The very darkness of prayer can become a place of resurrection.

A spirituality of subversion

The cave reminds us that not only did salvation spring from the depths of the earth, the Church too was an underground movement in more than one sense. Christians met and worshipped underground in the early centuries when facing persecution, in the catacombs of Rome and in the underground cities of Cappadocia. The Church was an underground movement also in the sense that it was deeply countercultural, holding to values quite different from society; it understood its mission in terms of being a hidden but effective agent of God's work, like yeast and salt (Matt. 13.33; 5.13).

The word 'subversive', from the Latin *subvertere*, literally means 'to turn from under, from below, from beneath'. The gospel itself is subversive as it throws up radical questions about society and its status quo, undermining its cultural norms. Recent scholars see Jesus as a subversive social revolutionary. He challenges both the power of Rome and the conventions of first-century Judaism with his message about the kingdom of God, where all are welcome and all are equal.[11] The kingdom of God represents a new way of living, a different path, an alternative vision for society, and the Sermon on the Mount reads like a radical manifesto.

The subversive nature of Jesus is seen very powerfully at the cross. He is crucified between two 'thieves' – this is the usual tame translation (Mark 15.27), but the Greek *lestes* denotes social bandits. Josephus tells us about such revolutionary activists who sought to undermine Roman domination by acts of sabotage or terrorism: the precursors of the Jewish Zealots and Sicarii. Jesus takes up the same word in his confrontation with the police in Gethsemane: 'Have you come out with swords and clubs to arrest me as though I were a bandit?' (Mark 14.48). But Jesus *is* a rebel in the eyes of Rome and crucifixion is the imperial reward for insurgents: the murderous insurrectionist Barabbas is meanwhile released. In contrast to the brutal strategy of the guerrilla fighters, Jesus becomes a rebel by peacefully advancing the reign of God. He is pinned to the cross, the violent alternatives to his left and right.

'God's foolishness is wiser than human wisdom' (1 Cor. 1.25). The early Church was a subversive community, for the apostles were described as 'people who have been turning the world upside down' (Acts 17.6). When the Church emerged, after the persecutions, into the Constantinian light of day, accommodations to culture and society were made: when Church and State fused in the Byzantine centuries, the Church forgot that her origins were from below, from the cave, her values discovered and forged in the darkness. The monks in their Judaean caves, as we shall see, formed a protest movement against such compromise.

A spirituality of hope

Palestinian Christians find themselves in a dark place right now. They are experiencing the gloom of the cave experience. The imprisoning siege of the Separation Barrier traps West Bankers with its vice-like grip on the territories. Those who live under continuing military occupation face the dark depression of the cave in the continuing heaviness and dehumanization that is part of everyday life. Palestinian Christians, in particular, face the darkness of being separated from their loved ones, as so many of the next generation emigrate to better prospects in the West. In 1948 Christians represented 18 per cent of the country's population; today the figure is about 1 per cent. In fact more than two-thirds of all Palestinian Christians now live outside the Holy Land, in their own experience of diaspora. In Jerusalem, we fear that Christian shrines will be left as museum pieces, with no living local congregations to pray in them.[12]

'The light shines in the darkness, and the darkness did not overcome it' (John 1.5). Christmas and Easter celebrations take on a new poignancy and power in the Holy Land. Christmas proclaims the triumph of divine light over human darkness: 'The people who walked in darkness have seen a great light; those who lived in a land of deep darkness – on them light has shined' (Isa. 9.2). The central feature of the Orthodox icon of the nativity is the pitch-black hole in the centre of the design, the dark deep cavern in the earth into which the divine Word descends. The icon depicts the powerful beam of light from the heavens penetrating the deepest darkness in the radiant and life-giving birth of the Redeemer.

Each Easter, from the darkness of the cave-tomb of Christ, Holy Fire breaks out in the Basilica of the Resurrection in Jerusalem. In the gloom of the tomb each Holy Saturday, a new light is kindled. It is passed out and quickly spread among thousands of pilgrims, each of whom holds a bundle of 33 candles representing the earthly life of Christ. The Holy Fire spreads like wildfire as the tapers become a radiant torch. The darkness is overcome and dispelled; the whole basilica is filled not only with light but with fire. The

Holy Fire: a powerful symbol that the darkness cannot quench the light of Christ; that the life and hope of the Risen One is an inextinguishable blaze. The Orthodox liturgy for Easter holds out hope: 'Now are all things filled with light;/ Heaven and earth, and the nethermost regions of the earth!'[13]

Questions for reflection

1 What is your experience of finding God in the darkness?
2 What does the Holy Land suggest to you about helping others in their darkness?
3 How do you find yourself responding to the idea of God as unknowable mystery?
4 In what sense do you see the Church as an underground, subversive community, asking difficult questions of your prevailing culture?
5 What signs of the activity of the Risen Christ can you discern in your community?

For further reading

I. Matthew, *The Impact of God: Soundings from St John of the Cross* (London: Hodder & Stoughton, 1995)

M. Matthews, *Both Alike to Thee: The Retrieval of the Mystical Way* (London: SPCK, 2000)

J. Murphy O'Connor, *The Holy Land* (Oxford: Oxford University Press, 1998)

H. Whybrew, *Risen with Christ* (London: SPCK, 2001)

Figure 5 Etched in rock: pilgrim memories in the Church of the Resurrection

5

The rock's questions

How far can I forgive?

'What do these stones mean?' The question resounds across the centuries. Joshua had set up 12 stones, taken from the Jordan riverbed, as a memorial to the miraculous crossing of the river and the entry of the people into the Holy Land. He anticipated that future generations would see the memorial and ask, 'What do those stones mean to you?', so that the memory of the event could be recalled. 'These stones shall be to the Israelites a memorial for ever' (Josh. 4.6, 7). In Old Testament times, it was common practice to mark a sacred site with a cairn or pile of rocks. A great stone marked the memory of the covenant's renewal at Shechem (Josh. 24.26). Jacob marked his experience of the ladder to heaven at Bethel with a stone pillar (Gen. 28.18) and he also set up a heap of rocks as a 'witness' to memorialize his covenant with Laban at Gilead (Gen. 31.45–51).

The Holy Land is full of commemorative rocks which evoke powerful memories, some very ancient, some recent, some raw and unhealed. Before the city of Jerusalem and its shrines were built, the landscape was dominated by two awesome rocks facing each other silently across the Tyropean Valley. To the east rose the monolith at the crest of the Ophel Ridge, a Canaanite high place of sacrifice before David's acquisition of it (2 Sam. 24.18–25). For Jews, this is Mount Moriah, the place of the offering of Isaac by Abraham, and marks the very Holy of Holies in Solomon's Temple. Today, this slab of stone, with all its diverse memories, lies beneath the Islamic Dome of the Rock, and for Muslims it celebrates the ascent of Muhammad into heaven; from it gushed the life-giving rivers at the dawn of creation. To the west there rises, above an ancient quarry, another mighty rock, saturated in blood, the limestone outcrop of Calvary or Golgotha: site of Roman torture and crucifixion, site of the death of Jesus. For Christians, this is the place where forgiveness is to be found.

Today throughout the Holy Land one sees latter-day Israeli memorials, mainly evoking the events of 1948. The road from Tel Aviv to Jerusalem passes a number of significant Jewish monuments. In the Judaean hills near Sha'ar HaGai one sees the stone edifice of the Machal Memorial to fallen soldiers; nearby, in the narrow gorge which was the scene of bitter and intense fighting in 1948, the rusted remnants of Israeli convoys memorialize the story. In Jerusalem, the sombre and heart-wrenching Yad Vashem museum preserves the memories of the darkest days of the Holocaust with the message, 'We shall never forget!' Nearby Mount Herzl is crowned with a range of stone memorials in its military cemetery.

Palestinian memorials are harder to discover. There is the silent witness of emptied villages, partially destroyed, walls still standing – one can see this on the highway to Jerusalem at Lifta. The broken remnants of long-deserted homes seem to shout out to those who pass by quickly on the highway, 'Do not forget the other side of 1948!' They bring another meaning to Christ's words: 'I tell you, if these were silent, the stones would shout out' (Luke 19.40). There are occasional Palestinian memorials to be found – for example, at Cana (Kaf Kana) – and these have increased in number since the 2000 Intifada, as the need not to forget has been recognized in the struggle to formulate a more robust Palestinian identity.

The stone memorials raise a host of questions with which we must wrestle. How do we remember collectively? 'Collective memory' is a term originating with Maurice Halbwachs (1877–1945), who not only highlighted the distinction between individual and societal memory (the private and the public) but also observed how 'living memory' shapes the formation of identity of peoples in the present.[1] Sometimes one hears the phrase 'let bygones be bygones' or 'the past is past'. Such attitudes cannot do justice to the deepest scars inflicted on peoples, wounds that still cry out for healing.

How is it possible for a people to remember the past without bitterness and recrimination? How can the Jews ever absolve Christians for perpetrating the events of the Crusades, with their brutal anti-Semitic violence? How can Jews forgive Christians for their culpability or implication in the Holocaust? Is it still too early for this to become possible, the bereavement still too raw? Only in recent years have survivors been able to talk about the experience at all. But the Holocaust lies as a heavy ache deep within the Israeli psyche, and has justified the establishing of the State of Israel amid violent confrontation. Today Israeli attitudes are marked by a deep mistrust of others, arising from the Holocaust, which sometimes reveals itself in abrasiveness or harshness towards non-Jews.

How can Palestinians, whether Christians or Muslims, ever forgive the Israelis for their past sufferings, dispossession and displacement, especially since these continue in the present? It is, perhaps, not an option being considered, for many Palestinians today are caught in an anxious depression as a result of the continuing occupation, deeply pained by being separated from their loved ones by the Separation Barrier, and fearful of what is to come.

What clues can we find in the Bible? In his 1986 Nobel Prize lecture *Hope, Despair and Memory*, Holocaust survivor Elie Wiesel reminds us of God's call to us to remember: 'No commandment figures so frequently, so insistently in the Bible.' The Old Testament is shaped by narratives of salvation history that recall God's deliverance and actions in the past. In particular, the Passover festival extends into the present the memory of the Exodus: 'This day shall be a day of remembrance for you. You shall celebrate it as a festival to the LORD; throughout your generations you shall observe it as a perpetual ordinance' (Exod. 12.14). The people are not to forget: 'Remember the long way that the LORD your God has led you these forty years in the wilderness, in order to humble you, testing you to know what was in your heart, whether or not you would keep his commandments' (Deut. 8.2). The book of Deuteronomy is especially insistent: 'Remember that you were a slave in the land of Egypt, and the LORD your God redeemed you'

(Deut. 15.15); 'Remember the days of old, consider the years long past; ask your father, and he will inform you; your elders, and they will tell you' (Deut. 32.7). And yet, despite this recurring call to remember, there is the occasional invitation to forget: 'Do not remember the former things, or consider the things of old' (Isa. 43.18).

Approaches to the past

Johann Baptist Metz, in his *Faith in History and Society*, explores two possible ways in which we can approach the past. One is the way of selective remembering. This is often the narrative of the victor and the powerful. Their history will celebrate the victories but not take account of the pain of the victims or the damage inflicted on others; rather it will blame the other. Selective memory acts as a filter, picks and chooses the parts to be recalled; it is often defensive of national pride and represents a denial of failure and of guilt. It reinforces stereotypes, demonizes the other as enemy and leads to continuing policies of revenge and retaliation.

Another approach is that of dangerous memory. In adopting this approach we will be prepared to recall the bad bits of the story, to acknowledge failures and mistakes, and attend to the wounds of the victims. We will look at the 'underside of history', taking responsibility rather than assigning blame. We will also be ready to offer a critique of the status quo, with uncomfortable and irritating questions for present policies and powers. Metz writes of dangerous memories that they are 'memories in which earlier experiences flare up and unleash new dangerous insights for the present. For brief moments they illuminate, harshly and piercingly . . . the banality of what we take to be "realism". They break through the canon of the ruling plausibility structures and take on a virtually subversive character'.[2] Such a reading of history requires vulnerability and humility, but it is the only approach that opens towards healing and forgiveness. The German theologian Geiko Müller-Fahrenholz writes of the possibilities of 'deep remembering': 'Processes of forgiveness . . . start by taking into account the victims of each victory . . . Forgiveness approaches history in a more inclusive way. It transcends the borderlines and recognizes that human beings are essentially the same here and there and everywhere.'[3]

The challenge of re-membering

The challenge of wholesome remembering is summed up in the word itself. 'Re-membering' can be seen as putting something together again that was broken and fragmented through time and history, restoring what was torn apart. Re-membering entails restoring wholeness to what was shattered, restoring relationships by a reciprocal process of recognizing the pain and fragmentedness, dislocation and disconnection on both sides. The task involves putting the missing pieces back into place. The alternative is not amnesia but dis-membering – giving in to processes that separate people one from another, allowing the tearing apart of the human family, allowing relationships to fall to pieces.

Re-membering takes courage and determination, for there are always insidious processes of fragmentation that work against it. It is vital for pilgrims to the Holy Land to attend to the two narratives, Palestinian and Israeli: two tellings of the same events, one despairing and the other triumphalist. In the context of the Holy Land, there is a double challenge to heal two dichotomies that are often kept separate: memory and hope, forgiveness and justice. Can these be put back together in a creative relationship?

Memory and hope

In Jerusalem the city and the mountain stand opposite each other as if poised for a dialogue between memory and hope: the stones of the city, with their blood-soaked memories, face across the Kidron valley the rock of the Mount of Olives, the mountain of eschatological hope, the mountain of the ascension of Christ (Acts 1.12) to which the Redeemer will one day return (Zech. 14.4; cf. Mark 13.26). Today the hillside is covered with tombs, Christian, Muslim and Jewish, awaiting in expectation the resurrection of the Day of the Lord. The very landscape speaks of the need for a dialectic and conversation between memory and hope, as Metz suggests, between looking back and looking forward, between the pain of the cross and the hope of ultimate renewal and resurrection, so that memories can be healed by the promise of new beginnings. As Jewish writer Marc Ellis puts it: 'The anchor of memory, especially the memory of violation and suffering, is waiting to be brought into a new relation with the wider public realm. Only by releasing one's hold on this memory, by forgiving through accepting a new promise, can one's horizons open up again.'[4]

Forgiveness and justice

Ellis writes that revolutionary forgiveness, the type that opens up opportunities for us to create a new future, is possible only when justice is done. 'It is in the ending of injustice and the journey toward a mutual and just future that forgiveness becomes revolutionary.'[5] If there is then a dialogue between memory and hope, between the cross and the resurrection, there also needs to be a dialogue between the twin themes of forgiveness and justice. As Carter Heyward puts it, in words very apposite to the situation between Israelis and Palestinians:

> People cannot simply 'forgive' – invite back into their lives on a mutual basis – those who continue to violate us, otherwise 'forgiveness' is an empty word. Forgiveness is possible only when the violence stops. Only then can those who have been violated even consider the possibility of actually loving those who once brutalized and battered them. Only then can the former victims empower the victimizers by helping them to realize their own power to live as liberated liberators, people able to see in themselves and others a corporate capacity to shape the future.[6]

Naim Ateek argues in *Justice and Only Justice*: 'To keep struggling against hate and to practice forgiveness need not mean abdicating one's rights or renouncing justice . . . It is part of our responsibility to ourselves and to God's people in the world to expose injustice.'[7]

'A time to gather stones, and a time to scatter'

These words, drawing on Ecclesiastes 3.5 remind us that while stones are gathered together in memorials, they are also used in other ways in the Holy Land. We see the throwing of stones as an act of retaliation or protest – children on the West Bank throwing stones at the threatening tanks of occupation, Ultra Orthodox at the edge of their very conservative Mea Shearim neighbourhood throwing stones at the police as a result of Sabbath disputes, Palestinians throwing stones on the Temple Mount when provoked by Jewish extremists entering the area to reclaim it for the building of the Third Temple.

But from the different traditions, we also see the use of stones in the healing of memory. In the cemeteries on the Mount of Olives, we see Jewish mourners placing a stone on the tomb of a loved one. Some tombs have many stones, some just a few. What do the stones denote? What stories they could tell, for behind each one is the mourner's own relationship to the past. Some stones are no doubt laid in thankfulness, honouring the dead. Others may be laid in deepest regret at opportunities missed. Some may be laid with a sense of seeking from the departed one forgiveness for unresolved arguments, harsh words or actions. The point is that the stone is brought to the place of the dead, and left there, on the tomb. The mourners do not take the stone home with them. There is a letting go . . . whatever pain the stone may represent, whatever heartache or trauma, is, in a sense, left there on the windswept hill, for time and tears to do their healing work. After prayers are offered and memories recalled, the mourner walks away, perhaps lighter in heart, into the future.

Another Jewish tradition is the opening, in the Rosh Hashanah festival, of the New Year with the practice of *tashlikh* (literally 'casting off'), in which stones, representing sins or regrets from the past, are symbolically cast into the water of a river or lake. This can be seen in the environs of Jerusalem, where Jews gather by streams or ponds for the ceremony. Here is a powerful symbol, as a new year begins, of letting go . . .

In the Christian tradition, John locates in Jerusalem's temple courts his story about the scribes and Pharisees taking up stones to throw in judgement at a woman caught in the act of adultery. Jesus' words echo across time to today: 'Let anyone among you who is without sin be the first to throw a stone' (John 8.7). Jesus demands that those who sit in judgement on others, those tempted to act in retaliation or revenge, first look to themselves, and into their own hearts. In the story, no one steps forward to cast a stone – all recognize that they are not blameless themselves. 'Neither do I condemn you,' says Jesus to the woman. 'Go your way.'[8]

Journey between the rocks

What significance does the Christian tradition in Jerusalem see in rocks or stones, that can help us explore the interplay between memory and forgiveness? Jesus himself is described as a *tekton* (Mark 6.3); often translated 'carpenter', the word can denote a stone-cutter or craftsman in rock. Jesus is reshaping the rocks of memory. We can get clues to a new approach to remembrance from the rock of Calvary itself. The paschal journey of Christ can be described as a 'journey between rocks', for it begins, in a sense, at the Rock of Agony in Gethsemane, now within the Basilica of All Nations, a rock drenched with the blood, sweat and tears of Jesus on the night of his Passion. As Luke tells us, 'His sweat became like great drops of blood falling down on the ground' (Luke 22.44).

The Way of the Cross, the Via Dolorosa, the road of sorrows itself, begins with rock. There is the evocative Prison of Christ (Greek Orthodox) with its gloomy and silent rock-hewn chambers cut into the limestone. Nearby we can still stand on the worn rock floor of the *Lithostrotos*, identified by some scholars as the Pavement of the Antonia Fortress. Extending from the *Ecce Homo* convent to the Church of the Flagellation, it recalls the place where Jesus is given his cross: 'Pilate . . . brought Jesus outside and sat on the judge's bench at a place called The Stone Pavement, or in Hebrew Gabbatha . . . He said to the Jews, "Here is your King!"'

(John 19.13, 14). The Way of the Cross is indeed a stony path, for it is marked by the several places where Jesus stumbled and fell into the dust under the weight of his cross. It is, in a sense, rocky ground, for it is strewn with the boulders and detritus of human pain and misunderstanding. It leads steeply uphill and today traverses the Old City of Jerusalem, gathering into itself the traumas and pains of the present.

It culminates in a rock that is scarred and shattered. The rock of Calvary itself may have been left standing amid the ancient quarry outside the city wall precisely because it was useless: a deep fracture running from its top into the earth indicates that it was unsuitable for use in building. It became a rejected rock. In Matthew's Gospel, Sinai-like earthquakes attend both the crucifixion and resurrection: 'The earth shook, and the rocks were split' (Matt. 27.51; see also 28.2). The rock of Calvary is indeed battered and bruised to this day: its deep scar and fracture speak powerfully of the woundedness and vulnerability of Christ. To see this at the top of Calvary (by the Greek altar) or at the foot of Calvary (the chapel of Adam) is to recall the pain, the bloodshed of Christ himself.[9] The first Christians, seeking to make sense of the event of Calvary, turned to the Hebrew Scriptures and there found texts which spoke of a rejected rock being used in God's rebuilding purposes for humanity: 'The stone that the builders rejected has become the chief cornerstone.' This verse from the Psalms (118.22) is used by different communities in the New Testament (it is quoted in Mark, Matthew and Luke in the Holy Week story, by Peter in his defence before the Jewish leaders in Acts 4.11, and by the writer of 1 Peter 2.7). Jesus is also understood as 'a stone one strikes against . . . a rock one stumbles over' (Isa. 8.14). But such a stone becomes the keystone in the new work, the new temple God is building, for a further text from Isaiah inspired the first Christians: 'See, I am laying in Zion a foundation stone, a tested stone, a precious cornerstone, a sure foundation' (28.16). This is quoted in Romans (9.33) and 1 Peter (2.4–6). The rock, then, is at once a memorial to the crucifixion and a pointer to a new future.

The rock of Calvary is part of a complex in the Church of the Holy Sepulchre that makes up 'the rock of our salvation'. The

Gospel accounts of the first Easter specifically mention rock. There is the tomb itself which Joseph of Arimathea had had cut into the rock-cliff (*petra*). There is the mighty rock or *lithos* with which the tomb of Christ was sealed, and which was blasted away in the course of the resurrection events (according to Matthew: parts are preserved in the antechamber of the tomb today in the Altar of the Angels). The empty cave of Christ's tomb, which Constantine had separated from the surrounding rock, is the timeless witness, the testimony to the reality of Christ's victory: 'The venerable and most holy memorial [*martyrion*] of the Saviour's resurrection' as Eusebius called it.

Thus the Way of the Cross is indeed a journey between the rocks. It leads from the rock of condemnation to the rock of salvation and to the rock of God's triumph. It is a journey through pain and deepest trauma to the new life and energy of the resurrection. The Way of the Cross has much to teach us about the healing of memory, about how we can remember trauma in a way that becomes redemptive. There is a double danger in the way people conduct the devotion of the Way of the Cross. It can become too narrowly pietistic, a matter between 'me and my Saviour', that is uprooted from contemporary realities in the wider world. Or it can become too historical, as if only marking an event distant in time, unrelated to the present. There are, perhaps, five ways we can walk the Via Dolorosa today, five prophetic ways that speak to the deep need for healing of memories, five approaches that can become transformative.

Healing *anamnesis*

Through the Way of the Cross we remember Christ's suffering, we commemorate his passage to death and beyond. We are recalling a historical event, but Christian liturgy enables a different kind of remembering: the Greek word for remembrance, *anamnesis*, in the institution of the Last Supper, denotes a making effective in the *now* the benefits of the *then*: the eucharistic remembrance releases into the present moment the power of the past.[10] We do not only remember Christ's Passion, we appropriate and receive Christ's hard-won graces and allow them to be transformative in our lives today. The words once uttered on Calvary resonate today in our situations of conflict: 'Father, forgive them' (Luke 23.34). Quickly we realize that the needful response to the Way of the Cross is one of repentance, the turning of hearts, the changing of attitudes. Stony hearts can become supple and responsive, and we can never be the same again if in penitence and humility we begin to learn the lessons of Christ's Passion.

Intercessory solidarity

Pascal wrote: 'Christ is in agony until the end of time.' In our very midst he suffers and rises today. Today he falls down into the dirt and dust in the experience of those whose human rights are trampled upon. Today he bleeds as blades of rejection are thrust into human flesh in warfare or violence. Christ walked the Way of the Cross not solely as 'Jesus of Nazareth', as if he were one solitary, private individual, but rather as the new Adam, as everyman/ everywoman, representing humanity itself. As Suffering Servant he embodied the destiny of a people (Isa. 53). As Son of Man he becomes a corporate, inclusive figure, encompassing all. He demands that we discern his very features today in the faces of those who suffer, for he calls us to find him in the broken and the downtrodden, to recognize his very presence in those who are hurting (Matt. 25).

This has particular resonance in the Holy Land. As Naim Ateek puts it: 'For Palestinian Christians, the experience of Golgotha is not a distant past or sad memory; it is part of everyday indignity and oppression. Our Via Dolorosa is not a mere ritualistic procession through the narrow streets of the old city of Jerusalem but the fate of being subjugated and humiliated in our own land.'[11] We can also recognize the experience of the Jewish people in the Holocaust as a Via Dolorosa. Christ carries the pains of all humanity in his Way of Sorrows.

The Gospels and tradition tell us that diverse human characters were caught up into the drama of the Way of the Cross – Mary, Simon of Cyrene, Veronica, the weeping women, the centurion. Winding its way through the very centre of the Old City of Jerusalem, today's Way of the Cross gathers into itself the heartaches and hopes of residents going about their daily business. Even within the Muslim quarter, it passes a Jewish yeshiva and witnesses Orthodox Jews rushing to pray at the Western Wall. It weaves its way like a thread through the city, like a healing stream through the very midst of communities. Arab women from the countryside sit on the ground selling sprigs of mint beside armed Israeli soldiers on duty. Tourists from all over the world mingle with pilgrims, peasants with craftsmen, businessmen with rubbish collectors: all the world is here! As we pray the Way of the Cross in our home church or context, the characters in the biblical story can alert us both to those who live physically in contemporary Jerusalem and to those across the globe who find themselves following a road of sorrows. The devotion becomes an act of solidarity and intercession that places us beside those who stumble and fall along a stony path today.

But intercession must lead to self-offering. It does not let you off the hook or allow you to think that your duty is done by praying. Self-offering is at the heart of intercession as we place ourselves at God's disposal for the outworking of his purposes.[12] In praying for healing we offer ourselves to be instruments of peace, for as Teresa of Avila reminds us, 'Christ has no body on earth but ours, no hands but ours, no feet but ours ... ours are the hands with which he is to bless and heal people now.' As Evelyn Underhill puts it: 'Real intercession is not merely a petition but a piece of work, involving costly self-surrender to God for the work he wants done on other souls.'[13] We find ourselves caught up into the very movement, current and flow of Christ's self-offering; interceding for others, we find ourselves offering ourselves for others.

Dangerous memory

We allow the Via Dolorosa to pose its subversive, disturbing questions to us today. Where are the Pilates today, the double-dealing authorities that are quick to judge and slow to comprehend? Who are the soldiers today who prod Jesus and humiliate him? Who will be a Simon of Cyrene today, helping others bear their cross, and sharing the bitter load? Who dare to be Veronicas today, stepping out on to the risky path to tenderly wipe the faces of those who suffer, a courageous action offering encouragement beyond words? And who will be the women of Jerusalem today (Luke 23.27–31) who will turn their tears of regret into tears of repentance? Who dares to be a person today who can be so deeply changed by the suffering and rising Jesus? Who will risk becoming empowered by him to forgive? Who will dare to open themselves to the disturbing graces of the resurrection?

Empowering paradox

The Way of the Cross emerges as a paradox which empowers us to act creatively in situations of conflict today. It is about divine foolishness that confounds the wisdom of the world (1 Cor. 1). Like the call in the Sermon on the Mount to love one's enemies (Matt. 5.44), it turns conventional attitudes of retaliation upside down and inside out. It is about divine weakness and brokenness that empowers us both to act and to react differently. The journey of the cross contains within itself a powerful momentum and dynamic which enable us to forgive others unilaterally. It imparts an energy that compels us to work for reconciliation. The scandalous block of Calvary, the rock to stumble over, becomes a stepping stone towards healing. 'We proclaim Christ crucified, a stumbling-block to Jews and foolishness to Gentiles, but to those who are the called . . . Christ the power of God and the wisdom of God' (1 Cor. 1.23, 24). The rock of Calvary becomes a launching pad for renewed mission, a springboard which catapults us back into the world and impels us towards the Other, even if the Other is hurting us.

Inspiring hope

See how people are changed on the Way of the Cross. It is a road marked by several life-changing conversions. Simon is taken out of himself into a risky involvement with the drama. The weeping women are shaken out of their tears of introversion towards an awareness of cosmic judgement. At the rock of Calvary itself, the Roman centurion moves from apathy to radical faith and insight, crying out: 'Truly this man was God's Son!' (Mark 15.39). Things look different the closer you get to Calvary. Perceptions shift, attitudes change as they come into interaction with the heart of Jesus.

The Way of the Cross these days has a fifteenth Station: the empty tomb. The journey of pain ends at the place of hope. It does not conclude with the body of a dead Jesus but with a dynamic rising unfettered Jesus, bursting from the tomb, going ahead to Galilee (Mark 16.7). Jesus is on the loose! He cannot be held down! He opens new futures for us. As Leonardo Boff puts it:

> The resurrection is a process that began with Jesus and will go on until it embraces all creation. Wherever an authentically human life is growing in the world, wherever justice is triumphing over the instincts of domination, wherever grace is winning out over the power of sin . . . wherever hope is resisting the lure of cynicism or despair, there the process of resurrection is being turned into a reality.[14]

Questions for reflection

1 Is forgiveness towards an injuring party possible without his or her prior repentance?
2 How do you understand the relationship between justice and forgiveness? Think of both personal and political examples.
3 'Let bygones be bygones.' Why is this an inadequate approach to the past?
4 What 'dangerous memories' are you aware of in the history of your own people? How do they affect present attitudes and policies?
5 How does the Way of the Cross resonate with your own experience?

For further reading

N. Ateek, *A Palestinian Christian Cry for Reconciliation* (New York: Orbis, 2008)

M. H. Ellis, *Revolutionary Forgiveness* (Waco, TX: Baylor University Press, 2000)

Figure 6 Battling for control: Crusader stronghold atop Tabor

6

The mountain's questions

How can I let go?

———•◆•———

Mount Tabor rises mysteriously and majestically, an intriguing oval shape, 2,000 feet above the Plain of Jezreel. Its thickly wooded sides, fragrant with pine, seem to point up to heaven itself. It is exposed to the elements, and often shrouded in low mist or cloud. Its transcendent quality accounts for its identification by the Byzantines as the place of the Transfiguration.

The accounts in the Gospels of the Transfiguration are full of awe. Matthew's account heightens the drama: the disciples fall down in fear at the vision of the radiant light, and Jesus needs to touch them to reassure them and lift them up (Matt. 17.1–8). Luke emphasizes that the reason why Jesus went up the mountain was to pray and that it was while he was praying that he was changed (Luke 9.28–36). Mark suggests that the theophany of the Transfiguration is about seeing the kingdom of God coming with power (Mark 9.1–8). All three accounts record Peter's reaction to the event: 'Then Peter said to Jesus, "Rabbi, it is good for us to be here; let us make three dwellings, one for you, one for Moses, and one for Elijah."' The evangelist adds the comment: 'He did not know what to say, for they were terrified' (Mark 9.5, 6).

Peter's struggle to be in control

What were Peter's motives in his plan to build three tents or tabernacles? Often in time of fear or stress one's true nature comes out. It seems that Peter wanted to regain mastery over circumstances that were unfolding without his scheming. He had lost the initiative. He needed to take charge and manage the event. Perhaps,

65

also, he needed to box in the mystery of the appearances, which was too great for his mind to grasp – he needed to get a handle on things, as we say. He needed to be able to take a grip on the situation, so he suggested that he would construct shelters in which things could be contained. Peter's heart was quaking with fear of the unknown. But above all, he simply needed to be in control.

This depiction of Peter's need to be in control resonates with other episodes where this side of his character emerges. At the Sea of Galilee, Peter the fisherman cannot accept, without arguing, Jesus' direction to put out into deep uncertain waters. 'We have worked all night long,' he protests (Luke 5.5). At Caesarea Philippi he takes Jesus aside and remonstrates with him, unable to accept an idea of a suffering Son of Man which goes well beyond his own narrow grasp of Jesus as Messiah (Mark 8.32). At the Last Supper, he at first refuses to be washed by Jesus – he wants things on his own terms. 'You will never wash my feet' (John 13.8). He strikes the high priest's servant in an effort to take charge (John 18.10). During the trials, he manifests his stubborn desire to stay in control by keeping his distance from Jesus (Luke 22). Jesus knows him: 'You used to fasten your own belt and to go wherever you wished' (John 21.18). His reaction on Tabor is 'in character'. It is as if he wants to manipulate the situation for his own ends.

What is God's response to Peter's request? It comes in the form of a dense mist or fog that envelops and enshrouds the disciples: 'A cloud came and overshadowed them' (Luke 9.34). The divine mystery was too big for any kind of tent. This reference to the overshadowing cloud evokes the theophany on Mount Sinai, where God appears in 'a thick cloud on the mountain' (Exod. 19.16). In his *Life of Moses*, Gregory of Nyssa (330–395), tracing the Christian path on the analogy of the Exodus, tells us that there are times when we need to allow ourselves to be overshadowed by the cloud of God's utter mystery:

> For leaving behind everything that is observed, not only what sense comprehends but also what the intelligence thinks it sees, the soul keeps on penetrating deeper until by the

intelligence's yearning for understanding it gains access to the invisible and the incomprehensible, and there it sees God. This is the true knowledge of what is sought; this is the seeing that consists in not seeing, because that which is sought transcends all knowledge, being separated on all sides by incomprehensibility as by a kind of darkness . . . Moses approached the dark cloud where God was.[1]

Gregory tells us that in prayer we need to let go of our controlling tendencies, which are expressed in our fixation with finding the right words for God, the right boxes to put him in. We need sometimes to silence our words and still our best efforts at achieving successful or satisfying prayer and rather expose ourselves to the unknowability of God: to let God be God, in all his transcendent and unspeakable mystery. The 'apophatic' approach to prayer, that learns to 'let go and let God', gives up the attempt to try to confine the divine within human categories and logic. This is both liberating for the Christian and also recognizes God's freedom and sovereignty. In the fifth century, Dionysius develops a similar theme:

Leave behind you everything perceived and understood, everything perceptible and understandable, all that is not and all that is, and, with your understanding laid aside, strive upward as much as you can toward union with him who is beyond all being and knowledge. By an undivided and absolute abandonment of yourself and everything, shedding all and freed from all, you will be uplifted to the ray of the divine shadow which is above everything that is.[2]

Peter must learn that to be a follower of Jesus is to be prepared to enter the place of risk, the place of Sinai-like danger, where there can be no controlling of a wild, unpredictable God, no domesticating the divine. He needs to be able to take a chance with God. It seems that the very reason Jesus leads his disciples up the mountain is precisely to enable them to encounter on the wind-blown hilltop the untamable God. Mount Tabor is a place of exposure to the divine, a place where Peter is invited to discover vulnerability, not the shielding safety of tents. Here he cannot hem himself in with self-protective tabernacles over which he holds the key. Peter needs to learn powerlessness and receptivity. The Eastern Church, where the mystery of the Transfiguration holds a central place in the liturgical calendar as the feast of the Metamorphosis, emphasizes that the divine energies streaming forth on Tabor necessitated a change in the disciples, not in Christ:

> The Transfiguration was not a phenomenon circumscribed in time and space; Christ underwent no change at that moment, even in his human nature, but a change occurred in the awareness of the apostles, who for a time received the power to see their Master as He was, resplendent in the eternal light of His Godhead. The apostles were taken out of history and given a glimpse of eternal realities. St Gregory Palamas says on his homily on the Transfiguration: 'The light of our Lord's Transfiguration had neither beginning nor end; it remained unbounded in time and space and imperceptible to the senses, although seen by bodily eyes . . . but by a change in their senses the Lord's disciples passed from the flesh to the Spirit.' To see the divine light with bodily sight, as the disciples saw it on Mount Tabor, we must participate in and be transformed by it, according to our capacity. Mystical experience implies this change in our nature, its transformation by grace.[3]

Gregory challenges us: dare we enter the divine light – even participate in the energies of God – if it might alter us, reshape us, make us different? Peter himself must be prepared to change: he encounters a light, beyond his controlling, which calls him to experience transfiguration himself. But he not only is dazzled by the unbounded light, he is also summoned to enter a disorientating cloud, which turns out to be the very place where God's voice will be heard (Luke 9.35). The image of the cloud, mysterious and uncircumscribable, itself becomes in spiritual writers a symbol of the God who cannot be grasped. The mystical fourteenth-century work *The Cloud of Unknowing* advises:

When you first begin, you find only darkness and as it were a cloud of unknowing. You don't know what this means except that in your will you feel a simple steadfast intention reaching out towards God . . . Reconcile yourself to wait in this darkness as long as is necessary, but still go on longing after him whom you love. For if you are to feel him or to see him in this life, it must always be in this cloud, in this darkness.[4]

The struggle for control: ancient and modern

Peter's attempt to take charge atop Mount Tabor was not the first time that there had been a struggle for control on the holy mountain. In fact all through history Tabor had been a strategic hilltop, overlooking the wide Jezreel valley (or plain) and commanding fine views of the Via Maris, the ancient route between Egypt and Assyria. At both ends of the valley, military strongholds kept watch from strategically important mountains. To the west, Megiddo from 3000 BC until recent times sought to dominate traders and invaders seeking entry into the valley: this is the biblical Armageddon, marked by the fortifications of many successive powers. Mount Moreh broods over the eastern end of the plain: here Gideon assembled his army against the Midianites (Judg. 7.1). Adjacent is Mount Gilboa, where Saul and Jonathan perished at the hands of the Philistines (1 Sam. 31), and nearby the Romans built a formidable military installation on Beth Shean's high ground, looming over the route from the Jordan valley. Tabor finds itself halfway along the Plain of Jezreel, and Josephus tells us that the Romans established a garrison at its crest, on the site that King Solomon himself had fortified. Both the Muslims and Crusaders built imposing fortresses on the summit of the holy mountain as they sought to command control of the area: a deep defensive ditch encircles the top of Tabor to this day.

But long before, as we turn back through the pages of the Old Testament, we see that Tabor marked a boundary in the allocation of land between the 12 tribes of Israel: it is where the territories of Zebulun and Issachar meet, according to the idealized history of the book of Joshua (Josh. 19). According to Judges 4 Deborah advised Barak to take position at Mount Tabor with ten thousand men. He swept down from the hilltop in a surprise attack when he saw the feared Canaanite general Sisera, king of Hazor, below. In the battle that ensued Sisera fled, and Jael welcomed him into a nearby tent, first offering him hospitality and respite, and then with a hammer driving a tent peg through his temple (Judg. 4.21). She was hailed as 'of tent-dwelling women most blessed' (5.24). The battle gave the Israelites their first access to the fertile and prosperous plain of Esdraelon after their 'conquest' of the land.

Mount Tabor poses its questions to the contemporary struggle for control in this land. Today a bitter struggle is being worked out on hundreds of hilltops across Israel/Palestine. The hilltops are again proving strategic. The question is: Who will be in control?

The Golan Heights, the hills that tower above the Sea of Galilee's eastern shore, were occupied by Israel in 1967 precisely because of their strategic significance, overlooking the Syrian enemy. Another mountain area of strategic importance to Israel is the hills of the north-western edge of the occupied territories, which lie across the valley from Tel Aviv airport. There is a deep fear that Palestinian attacks might be launched on the airport from this area, so it is now firmly in Israeli lands and peopled with settlements; nearby, 20,000 settlers live in the Jewish city of Ariel which has been constructed on confiscated land. Right across the Palestinian territories, hilltops have been appropriated by Israelis, by the military and by economic and religious settlers. One hundred and sixty-eight officially sanctioned and subsidized settlements have been established since 1967; there are also 102 outposts.[5] The Jewish settlements are not temporary arrangements, as the name might suggest, but constitute vast hilltop housing estates built of concrete and rock with populations approaching half a million. A network of Zionist settler youth groups is called 'Hilltop Youth'. The significance of the hilltops is easy to see. They command wide views. They are easier to defend in case of attack. But above all, they dominate the landscape and send out a powerful message about who has mastery over the land.

Since the Oslo accords of the 1990s, the occupied Palestinian areas of the West Bank have been subjected to three types of control. Area A, 17 per cent of the West Bank, including the main Palestinian towns of Jericho, Ramallah and Nablus, has been granted limited Palestinian civil administrative autonomy with all boundaries controlled by Israel; these communities are like islands in a sea of Israeli domination. Area B covers certain populated rural areas; this has some Palestinian administration but overall Israeli control. Area C, representing 40 per cent of the West Bank, contains all the Israeli settlements with their access roads; these are under sole Israeli authority. Area C also includes almost all the Jordan valley and the Judaean desert. Israel maintains supremacy over the land, roads, water, airspace, external security and borders for the entire occupied territory. Forty per cent of the total area of the West Bank is taken up by Israeli infrastructure: settlements, the Separation Barrier, access roads, closed military areas and checkpoints, which combine to tighten the Israeli grip of control across the Palestinian territories.

The Israeli quest for power and domination in this land needs to be understood against the background of the Holocaust – the experience of utter powerlessness, the unspeakable torture of being victims in the hands of a death-dealing tyrant. 'Never again' is the Israeli watchword. The present-day threats to Israel's security from different directions also help us understand Israelis' profound mistrust of others, which lies behind the struggle for control. But sadly it resonates with domination systems from the past, and reminds us, in some ways, of the background to Jesus' ministry. When he chose to embody his message in terms of the kingdom of God, he found a concept that would bring him in direct opposition to the kingdom or power of his day, that of Rome, administered in Palestine by the cruel and paranoid Herod the Great and then by the brutal Pontius Pilate. It was an oppressive military domination that exploited the ordinary people through taxation and heavy-handed policing. Jesus proclaimed the kingdom or rule of God as an alternative, a different vision, based on reconciliation and social justice.[6] The kingdom is not to be defined territorially: it is a realm open to all.

When we turn to the Old Testament, we discover a theology of the land that is emphatic: 'The land is mine,' says the Lord. The gift of the land is described repeatedly as an 'inheritance' – something to be shared, not grasped at. The Hebrews are stewards and tenants in God's land. 'The land shall not be sold in perpetuity, for the land is mine; with me you are but aliens and tenants' (Lev. 25.23). The Israelites could not do with the land as they might choose. As an inheritance, it could only be used in ways faithful to the moral imperatives of social justice and compassion. Thirty-six times in the Hebrew Scriptures the Jews are called not to dominate but to be compassionate to strangers and aliens. 'The alien who resides with you shall be to you as the citizen among you; you shall love the alien as yourself, for you were aliens in the land of Egypt' (Lev. 19.34). As Stephen Sizer observes: 'The Land is never at the disposal of Israel for its national purposes. Instead it is Israel who is at the disposal of God's purposes.'[7] Once again, it is a question of 'who is in charge?'

Did Peter, for his part, ever learn to relinquish control? Did he ever move from needing to be in control, to a place of vulnerability and openness? Perhaps in John 21 we see a different Peter emerging. At the sight of the Risen Jesus by the water's edge he is prepared to leave his boat – symbol of his self-confidence and place of personal security. Jumping into the water to see Jesus, he sets aside his own agenda and his own set of priorities, represented in his stubborn return to fishing. Significantly, in seeing the Risen Jesus, Peter cries out, 'It is the Lord!' (John 21.7). He is recognizing, finally, the lordship and sovereignty of someone other than himself. In accepting the triple commission given to him by Jesus, Peter allows Jesus to set his agenda, at last.

Questions for reflection

1 What is needed to allow us to move from being in control to being a place of vulnerability and openness before God? What steps do we need to take to be able to 'let go and let God'?

2 What do you make of Paul's words, 'Whenever I am weak, then I am strong' (2 Cor. 12.10)?

3 How can the political need to be 'in control' be transformed into an attitude of mutual trust and openness to the Other?

4 How far can you identify with Peter's experience? What lies behind the need to be in control?
5 What other examples in the Bible of utter surrender to God can you recall?

For further reading

G. M. Burge, *Jesus and the Land: The New Testament Challenge to 'Holy Land' Theology* (London: SPCK, 2010)

J. D. Crossan, *God and Empire* (San Francisco: HarperOne, 2007)

T. L. Donaldson, *Jesus on the Mountain* (Sheffield: JSOT Press, 1985)

W. A. Meninger, *The Loving Search for God: Contemplative Prayer and the Cloud of Unknowing* (New York: Continuum, 1997)

S. R. Sizer, *Christian Zionism: Road-map to Armageddon?* (Downers Grove, IL: InterVarsity Press, 2005)

Figure 7 Taking the waters: extraction from Galilee

7

The lake's questions

How far can I share?

———•◆•———

'O Sabbath rest by Galilee, O calm of hills above.' The very name of Galilee evokes a myriad of memories from the Gospels: the call of the disciples from their occupation as fishermen, near the harbour at Capernaum (Mark 1.16–20); Jesus walking on water (Mark 6.45–52); Jesus calming the storm (Mark 4.35–41); the appearance of the risen Christ by the lakeside (John 21.1–14). Jesus taught by the shore and from the lake (Mark 4.1). The verdant, lush hills around Galilee and waterside villages like Bethsaida and Magdala formed the context for the Galilean ministry. The lake was life-giving – teeming with fish (John 21.11) – and sustained many livelihoods.

Melting snows from Mount Hermon give rise to abundant streams which constitute the three tributaries of the River Jordan – the Dan, the Banias and the Hatzbani. To this day rich vegetation and an astonishing range of bird life flourish along their banks. The lake itself, while 13 miles long and 7 miles wide, is only 150 feet deep. It is a lake of many moods – its calm contemplative waters can be quickly transformed into the frightening waves of a violent storm, fuelled by winds rushing down from the valleys. It is also a lake of many colours: inky blackness becomes tinged with orange at dawn, while in daytime the lake can either be a sparkling, dazzling mirror reflecting the Middle Eastern sun or, at times, a dark, forbidding blue. At sunset, a mist may cling to the surface, the colour of which can change from shimmering turquoise to pale yellow, blending into dusk's red hues before the velvet of night returns.

The pilgrim to the Holy Land comes across the issue of water at every turn. An itinerary in the Holy Land will include many encounters with wells: Mary's well at Nazareth, the well of the vineyard at Ein Karem, Jacob's well at Shechem (present-day Nablus). Pilgrims are exhorted, especially in the summer months, always to carry water – dehydration can be a real problem. Pilgrims will visit archaeological sites, such as Masada and Caesarea Maritima, that include many cisterns and aqueducts. Pilgrims will realize, too, the significance of water in Judaism and Islam. At such places as the Southern Wall excavations in Jerusalem and at Qumran one sees the Jewish *mikveh*; often labelled 'ritual bath', it is the pool where physical purity and cleanliness are attained before prayer can begin. Similarly one sees the Islamic *sabeel*, or fountain, and the ritual ablution pools near the Dome of the Rock where worshippers cleanse themselves before prayer. In Muslim tradition the rivers of creation bubble up beneath the great Rock of the Noble Sanctuary. Throughout the Old City one sees beautiful but neglected Ottoman drinking fountains set in ornate recesses. Jerusalem itself was established where it was precisely because of water, and the very designation 'Zion' may derive etymologically from 'thirsty place' or 'arid place' – a significant derivation physically and spiritually. It was built by the Gihon spring (2 Chron. 32.30), located outside the city wall, and Hezekiah constructed a tunnel to channel its waters within the city's parameters during the period of the Assyrian threat. Psalm 46 rejoices: 'There is a river whose streams make glad the city of God.'

The physicality of water

It is easy to romanticize the Sea of Galilee, as in Whittier's hymn, but today it has a very functional use, as one of Israel's three major water reserves – it is the country's largest reservoir. Via the National Water Carrier its waters are pumped down to the Negev desert for irrigation. Israeli creativity and scientific technology, which invented the drip system for irrigation, have transformed arid areas into fertile farmlands, watered from the Sea of Galilee. But today the waters of the lake are alarmingly low and the water line is receding at a dramatic rate, the result of unusually light snows on Hermon, meagre rains and overpumping. The steps of an ancient landing stage beside the Church of St Peter's Primacy at Tabgha, which until the 1980s went down into the water, evoking the story of John 21, now find themselves some 200 metres from the shoreline. The water level at the time of writing is just 75 centimetres above the 'black line', the limit of water extraction, and 4.5 metres (15 feet) below the maximum desired level. Today the receding waters of the Sea of Galilee symbolize very dramatically a major crisis facing Israel/Palestine – the desperate clamour for water. Jeremiah's ancient words seem so contemporary:

> Judah mourns and her gates languish;
> they lie in gloom on the ground,
> and the cry of Jerusalem goes up.
> Her nobles send their servants for water;
> they come to the cisterns;
> they find no water,
> they return with their vessels empty.
> They are ashamed and dismayed
> and cover their heads,
> because the ground is cracked.
> Because there has been no rain on the land
> the farmers are dismayed;
> they cover their heads.   (Jer. 14.2–4)

Galilee's waters are supplemented only by the coastal aquifer and the mountain aquifer, which lies deep in the Palestinian West Bank territory. The newly built Separation Barrier cuts deep into the West Bank area at Ariel in order for the Israelis to wrest control of the mountain aquifer from the Palestinians. Of the water from this aquifer, the Israelis use 83 per cent and the Palestinians 17 per cent. The Israelis use four times the amount per capita that the Palestinians are permitted.[1] In the summer months, when reserves are low, the Israeli water company Mekorot closes valves supplying Palestinian villages on the West Bank in order to safeguard supplies for the settlers. The Jewish settlers fill their swimming pools, wash their cars and water their lawns, while just a couple of miles away Palestinian villages may be denied water for essential use in cooking and sanitation, water vital for their mere survival.

The struggle for water is ancient in this land. The Old Testament itself, in two stories about disputes over water, suggests ways in which resources can be shared equitably. In Genesis 21.25–34 we read of Abraham's argument with the Canaanite warlord Abimelech, whose servants seized control of a well of water Abraham was using. Abraham resolves the dispute and avoids further conflict by entering into a covenant with Abimelech, sealing the agreement by his gift to him of seven lambs, which gives the well the name 'Beersheba', meaning 'the well of the oath'. Some time later Abraham's son Isaac also comes face to face with Abimelech, in a passage which repays close study, Genesis 26.14–33. It vividly illustrates the scramble for water in this thirsty land. Isaac's servants dig a well but Abimelech's herdsmen protest in words that are heard today in this same land: 'The water is *ours*' (Gen. 26.20, emphasis added). Isaac refuses to give in to fear and intimidation and moves on, sinking another well at a distance (but no doubt using the same underground water table). Ultimately he enters into a covenant with Abimelech (Gen. 26.31), a relationship based on mutual respect and mutual interest – former foes sit and eat and drink (water?) together as they seal a pact and exchange oaths. That same day Isaac's servants come to him rejoicing and say, 'We have found water!' As Isaac observes (Gen. 26.22), there is room in the land for both groups, and there is enough water for all. The lessons shout to us from ancient Beersheba: the way forward from dispute and struggle is by way of covenant and mutual trust.

The spirituality of water

Water has become an evocative symbol of the spiritual life. John's Gospel mentions water in almost every chapter – intermingling its physical necessity with its spiritual significance. Water is needed for the Jewish rites of purification (2.6) and for Christian baptism (1.26, 31; 3.23). Jesus says that 'no one can enter the kingdom of God without being born of water and Spirit' (3.5). The Pool of

Bethesda to the north of the Temple serves as a healing sanctuary (5.7), while the Pool of Siloam to the south of the Temple also becomes a place of restoration (9.7). Water at a wedding becomes the wine-symbol of Christ's Passion (2.1–11). The water of the lake becomes a pathway for the Son of God (6.16, 19) who can calm its storms. Peter is later to jump into the water of Galilee and swim to Jesus (21.7). Jesus takes water and pours it out to wash the disciples' feet (13.5), a radical symbol of the serving of others.

The two most significant references to water are found in chapters 4 and 7. To the woman drawing supplies at Jacob's well, Jesus says: 'If you knew the gift of God . . . you would have asked him, and he would have given you living water . . . those who drink of the water that I will give them will never be thirsty. The water that I will give will become in them a spring of water gushing up to eternal life' (4.10, 14). Jesus promises a Spirit who quenches our deepest thirst, an inner geyser, welling up to eternal life. And so chapter 7 of John's Gospel gives us the dramatic cry of Christ:

> On the last day of the festival, the great day, while Jesus was standing there, he cried out, 'Let anyone who is thirsty come to me, and let the one who believes in me drink. As the scripture has said, "Out of the believer's heart shall flow rivers of living water."' Now he said this about the Spirit, which believers in him were to receive; for as yet there was no Spirit, because Jesus was not yet glorified.   (John 7.37–39)

The great Jewish festival of Tabernacles, with its vision of the river of God, forms the context of this event. Jesus attends the temple liturgy at which Ezekiel's vision (ch. 47) is proclaimed to the pilgrims: a spring of God's generous blessing bursting forth from under the altar of the Temple and spilling out to bring renewal to the whole world. The water grows deeper and deeper as Ezekiel follows the line of the river from the holy city, out and into the desert. At first the prophet is able to wade in the water, but soon it comes up right to his waist, so he has to swim in the river of God's blessing. The Tabernacles festival reached a climax when, on the last day, in a solemn ceremony celebrating this vision, waters from the Pool of Siloam were carried up to the Temple in a golden vessel, and poured out as a sign of God's blessing in 'the Age to Come'. Jesus is watching this ritual when he cries out his urgent, awesome promise. You do not have to wait until the Last Day! With Jesus' glorification on the cross the Spirit will be unleashed as an overflowing stream to renew all of creation. John links the gift of the Spirit to the paschal mystery. At the crucifixion, a fountain of eternal life is opened for humanity: as his side is pierced, blood and water stream out (John 19.34; cf. 1 John 5.6–8). After Jesus is glorified on the cross, the Spirit can gush forth.

When Jesus echoes Ezekiel's prophecy and makes his glorious promise, what does he mean? How can the Spirit come to us as a stream of living water and flow in us and out through us? The promise resonates with four aspects of the Spirit's work. First, Jesus alludes to the energy of the Spirit. He is talking of the cascade of the Spirit, the movement of the Spirit, the empowering of the Spirit, his energy within us. Second, he speaks of an inflow and an overflow. The Spirit comes to us and then, bubbling up like a mountain brook, streams out to others. The geography of the Holy Land echoes this message: where there is an inflow but no outflow, a receiving but no giving, we find the Dead Sea, in which all life dies. But where there is the healthy inflow and outflow of the Jordan we find the life-giving Sea of Galilee, teeming with life. Third, Jesus alludes to the cleansing of the Spirit, the washing away of our mistakes. Part of the work of the Spirit is to apply to us the benefits of the cross, which makes possible a river of forgiveness and a radical new start for those who are penitent. Fourth, Jesus is talking about the renewing and refreshing grace of the Spirit. As sparkling, living water invigorates and enlivens weary bodies, so the Spirit makes us new, replenishing and restoring parched souls: this is the healing grace of the Spirit, echoing Ezekiel's vision of trees with leaves for healing thriving alongside the riverbank (Ezek. 47.12).

In the glorious promise of the river of God, Jesus suggests three steps the disciples need to take: 'If any thirst, let them come to me and drink. Out of their heart will flow rivers of living water.'

First, they must acknowledge and recognize their thirst for the Spirit. Second, they need to come to Jesus the giver of the Spirit and place themselves in expectant relation to him. Third, they are invited to drink and receive afresh the living water. In our prayer we can take these three steps. In prayer, we can thirst, come to Jesus and drink, receiving afresh the Spirit of God.

As winter springs replenishing Galilee's reserves become a symbol of God's overflowing grace, so in the history of Christian spirituality the image of water has inspired countless teachers of prayer. Let us look at two examples, drawn from east and west.

St Symeon the New Theologian (949–1022) is one of the Eastern Church's greatest mystics. He emphasizes the necessity of personal encounter with the divine, and tells his own story:

> He led me by the hand as one leads a blind man to the fountain head, that is, to the holy scriptures and to Your divine commandments . . . One day when I was hurrying to plunge myself in this daily bath, You met me on the road, You who had already drawn me out of the mire. Then for the first time the pure light of Your divine face shone before my weak eyes . . . From that day on, You returned often at the fountain source, You would plunge my head into the water, letting me see the splendour of Your light . . . One day when it seemed as though You were plunging me over and over again in the lustral waters, lightning flashes surrounded me. I saw the rays from Your face merge with the waters; washed by these radiant waters, I was carried out of myself.[2]

For Symeon, the image of the waters becomes a powerful metaphor of the spiritual life, bespeaking the unfathomable resources of the Spirit, and God's generosity in sharing his gifts. In the West, St Teresa of Avila (1515–82) writes of the Prayer of Quiet using the picture of the fountain:

> Let us suppose that we are looking at two fountains, the basins of which can be filled with water . . . These two large basins can be filled with water in different ways: the water in the one comes from a long distance, by means of numerous

conduits and through human skill; but the other has been constructed at the very source of the water and fills without making any noise. If the flow of water is abundant, as in the case we are speaking of, a great stream still runs from it after it has been filled; no skill is necessary here, and no conduits have to be made, for the water is flowing all the time. The difference between this and the carrying of the water by means of conduits is, I think, as follows. The former corresponds to the spiritual sweetness which, as I say, is produced by meditation. It reaches us by way of the thoughts; we meditate upon created things and fatigue the understanding; and when at last, by means of our own efforts, it comes, the satisfaction which it brings to the soul fills the basin, but in doing so makes a noise, as I have said.

To the other fountain the water comes direct from its source, which is God, and, when it is His Majesty's will and He is pleased to grant us some supernatural favour, its coming is accompanied by the greatest peace and quietness and sweetness within ourselves.[3]

In this passage from *Interior Castle*, written in 1577, St Teresa suggests there are two ways of receiving the water of God. Either we can stand at a distance from the fountain of God, and receive the water of the Spirit as it were mediated through man-made and lengthy aqueducts and conduits, miles of pipelines of active, often noisy, talkative prayer. This in fact creates a distance from the fountain. Or we can stand very close to the fountain of God, quieten our spirit, and change our prayer from an active, thinking and striving style to a more receptive, passive, drinking-in style. In what Teresa calls 'the Prayer of Quiet', we can drink directly and immediately of the river of the Spirit bubbling up in front of us. How close, she asks, are you to the fountain?

Dare we share?

'O Sabbath rest by Galilee, O calm of hills above'? Today's Sea of Galilee is often experienced by pilgrims as a tranquil and soothing environment, after the hustle and stress of the city of Jerusalem. The effect is restorative and healing. But it was not always so: the pilgrim has to be reminded that the Galilee of Jesus' time was a place of increasing poverty, that it witnessed an increasing polarization between rich and poor. An exploitative and grabbing urban elite resided in the affluent cities of Tiberias and Sefforis, while in their humble lakeside villages Jewish peasants barely eked out a living. Peter Walker paints a dramatic picture: 'The Palestine in which Jesus grew up was politically red-hot. The tension between the Jews and Roman rulers was increasing... Jesus found himself in a context that was like a tinderbox waiting to go up in flames.'[4]

Among the root causes of this simmering discontent was the breakdown in equitable sharing of resources. Peasant farmers, who had garnered their harvests on family plots of land since time immemorial, were now forced to sell their ancestral holdings to pay heavy taxes. They then became tenants on their own land, and were further crippled by the burden of rent. Matthew's version of the Lord's Prayer reflects this crisis: 'Forgive us our debts, as we also have forgiven our debtors' (Matt. 6.12). While Luke spiritualizes this into 'forgive us our sins', the first Gospel preserves the blunt physicality of material debt. Into this situation comes Jesus with a radical message about the kingdom of God where all are equal and valued. At Tabgha, the place where seven streams empty into Galilee, and close to the present Sapir water-pumping site of Israel's National Water Carrier, tradition locates an inspirational story about the sharing of meagre reserves: Christ's feeding of the five thousand. Andrew asks: 'There is a boy here who has five barley loaves and two fish. But what are they among so many people?' (John 6.9). Miracles happen when resources are shared. To share is not to lose, but to gain.

Questions for reflection

1 Jesus asks the Samaritan woman, 'Give me a drink' (John 4.7). Jesus says, 'Whoever gives even a cup of cold water to one of these little ones in the name of a disciple – truly I tell you, none

of these will lose their reward' (Matt. 10.42). How prepared are you to share your physical resources?

2 What spiritual resources do you have to share with those who are spiritually thirsty in your midst?

3 How aware are you of the physical thirst in the peoples of the Holy Land?

4 How aware are you of your own spiritual thirst?

5 In what ways do you experience the Holy Spirit as 'living water'?

For further reading

J. Selby, *Water, Power and Politics in the Middle East: The Other Israeli-Palestinian Conflict*, Library of Modern Middle East Studies (London: I. B. Tauris, 2004)

J. S. Starr, *Covenant Over Middle Eastern Waters* (New York: Henry Holt & Co., 1995)

Figure 8 Destruction and construction: Mamilla's enclosure fence hides the building site

8

The garden's questions

How can I embrace the struggle?

At the centre of the Bible, the rich poem of the Song of Songs invites us to explore two themes in connection with the garden. First, it invites us to enjoy a spontaneous delight in the beauty of creation and to rediscover a sacramental approach to the world. In this Wisdom literature, the garden becomes a meeting place for lovers, place of the tryst, the bride and groom celebrating their love. It resonates with a key life-affirming undercurrent in Jewish spirituality, the goodness and givenness of creation: 'The earth brought forth vegetation: plants yielding seed of every kind, and trees of every kind bearing fruit with the seed in it. And God saw that it was good' (Gen. 1.12). Indeed, the most typical form of Jewish prayer is the *berakhah*, the blessing of God for his gifts: 'Blessed are you, Lord God, King of the universe.' The sacramentality of creation is celebrated throughout Christian spirituality; in their commentaries on the Song of Songs, writers such as Gregory of Nyssa, Bernard of Clairvaux and even the Puritan John Owen, note how physicality and materiality point to spirituality, and how the love of bride and bridegroom speaks of Christ's love for his Church.

But the Song of Songs also invites us to a second, darker theme in connection with the garden: the garden emerges as the place not only of personal communion, but also of intense struggle. In heartbreak, the bridegroom finds 'a garden locked is my sister, my bride' (4.12). When the bride awakes from slumber, she finds that her lover has gone: 'I sought him, but did not find him; I called him, but he gave no answer' (5.6). The garden becomes a place of separation, of communion disrupted, of love unrequited. It

87

becomes a place of unanswered questions: 'What is your beloved . . . ?' (5.9). 'Which way has your beloved turned . . . ?' (6.1). The poem ends with the bride's agonized cry: 'O you who dwell in the gardens, my companions are listening for your voice; let me hear it. Make haste, my beloved' (8.13, 14).

This double theme, of presence and absence, of communion and struggle, alerts us to the ambiguity and paradox of the garden and prepares us for the three gardens that the visitor to Jerusalem is likely to enter. Each speaks in its own way of the theme of struggle. Indeed, Jerusalem could be called the tale of three gardens.

The primordial garden

Around the awesome building of the Dome of the Rock, which tops the mighty rock of Mount Moriah, lie gardens which cover a large part of what Muslims call 'the Noble Sanctuary' and Jews call the 'Temple Mount'. It is the biggest open space in the Old City of Jerusalem, providing respite from the crowds and a welcome sense of spaciousness after the confinement of the narrow alleys. These gardens consist of olive groves and a planting of conifer trees, and offer wonderful shade on a hot day. But they are not planted for such relief but for recreation, or rather, re-creation. They are there to make a theological statement about our beginning and our end, and to remind us of the spiritual struggle in between. In the Islamic tradition, the sacred rock beneath the Dome is the foundation stone of creation and, as we recalled, the first rivers of the world welled up from beneath it. This is the centre of the world and the burial place of Adam and Eve. This is the location of Paradise itself.

In Muslim spirituality the theme of a garden of Eden, a Paradise to be regained, makes frequent appearances. The story of Eden, as recounted in the Qur'an, depicts Adam in his dignity as viceregent, literally God's deputy king on earth. As Genesis portrays Adam and God walking together in the cool of the day, an image of the primordial communion with God to which humanity is called, so the Qur'an celebrates the garden of delights and speaks often of the Paradise to be regained after death and after judgement. In all three traditions there is the understanding that the fall of Adam, who represents all of us, was due to his pride and ego. Whether understood as history or as story, as event or parable, the struggle in the garden is humanity's perennial struggle: preferring ego over God, choosing the way of self-determination over God's guidance.

The Qur'an promises the faithful the blessings of a Paradise regained. It speaks of 'gardens underneath which rivers flow' (II.25), 'the shelter of plenteous shade' (IV.57), 'forgiveness and a generous provision' (VIII.4). It speaks of Paradise as the longing of humanity: 'all that your souls desire' (XLI.31). In the Sufi tradition, 'to enter the garden' is to actualize the purposes of creation.[1] Muslim mystics contrast the image of the garden with that of the fire. 'Their Garden is the turning of their hearts toward God, and their Fire is the turning of their hearts away from him.'[2] Each day the individual has to choose between the garden and the fire: 'Your heaven and hell are within yourself: Look inside! See furnaces in your liver, gardens in your heart.'[3] While fire represents selfish passion, the garden denotes the choice of submission and obedience to God's will.

Thus a walk in the gardens of the Noble Sanctuary recalls both Adam's struggle with the serpent, and his struggle with himself. The gardens remind us of our calling and destiny: to walk again in Eden. The nearby arches, which frame the area around the Dome of the Rock on four sides, represent the scales of judgement – accountability to God is a strong theme in Islam. Opposite the gardens is the eschatological mountain, the Mount of Olives, which stands as a continual reminder to the worshipper of the End Time. Thus the visitor walks between the garden and the mountain, between Eden and End, between the start and the finish: this is where we live and where we seek to enjoy even now a foretaste of Paradise, our primordial home. Here below we face the daily struggle and the daily choice: the possibility of re-entering the garden, even now. This is the greater jihad or inner, spiritual struggle of which Islam speaks. A lesser jihad is the external, military combat, but the greater jihad is the struggle we have with ourselves and within ourselves, that we might overcome disobedience against God and return to Adam's state before his fall, which is the place of surrender before God – the meaning, of course, of the word Islam itself.

The political garden

Just to the east of Jerusalem's Great Synagogue is the biggest park in the new city. Named Independence Park by the Israelis in 1967, it provides acres of precious grass and trees, with a cooling stream at its centre. It is a magnet for people throughout the year, and especially on lazy summer afternoons. In part of the park, the Simon Wiesenthal Center of Los Angeles is planning to construct two massive buildings, a Museum of Tolerance and a Museum of Human Dignity, with the aim of promoting tolerance among Jewish populations in Israel, including the various communities of the Diaspora who now live here. However, the site has become a place of bitter political struggle, for the very same area contains the ancient Muslim Mamilla cemetery. In the cemetery are interred, it is believed, the companions of the Prophet himself, as well as the fallen soldiers of Saladin, who led the Muslim recapture of Jerusalem from the Crusaders in 1187. It was then used as a Muslim burial place for 800 years until 1927, when the Muslim Supreme Council designated it a historical site to be respected and honoured.

Since 1948 hundreds of Islamic tombs within this area have been defaced and destroyed, and bulldozers are poised to complete the almost total obliteration of graves and their markers. The eradication of history is taking place, and part of Jerusalem's heritage will be lost for ever. It is a supreme irony that the acts of vandalism and destruction carried out against the Muslim dead are being carried out in the name of a Jewish Museum of Tolerance. The garden has become an ideological battlefield over human rights and human respect. An unlikely Muslim–Jewish initiative is seeking to halt construction. Members of an Ultra Orthodox organization which fights against the destruction of Jewish tombs, have been persuaded to join the fray by trying to get the site declared ritually impure under Jewish law, due to the presence of Muslim dead. But an Israeli court has recently authorized the demolition of 200 recently renewed tombstones, while an appeal to UNESCO has proved fruitless.[4]

At the time of writing, a variety of sounds are to be heard in the once-silent graveyard ... the innocent laughter of children playing, and the noise of construction machines working in an area closed off to the public. This garden raises in a symbolic way a number of issues behind the Israeli–Palestinian conflict: the use of power by the conquering force, the question of whether mutual respect between different peoples and different religions is possible. It is indeed a garden of struggle.[5]

The paschal garden

How Jesus loved the Garden of Gethsemane on the lower slopes of the Mount of Olives. Its cool shady areas and ancient olive trees – the garden's very name means 'oil press' – give shelter from rain and sun. We know from the Gospels (Luke 22.39) that Jesus often went to this grove, either to teach, or simply to spend time with his disciples. But on the night we call Maundy Thursday, the garden of fellowship became a place of struggle ... a spiritual battleground. Our third garden is wet, not only with the night dew, but with the tears of Christ. 'Jesus offered up prayers and supplications, with loud cries and tears' (Heb. 5.7). William Lane tells us: 'The reference to "cries and tears" describes prayer in a setting of crisis.'[6] Christ, a second Adam, finds himself in a garden on the eve of his Passion, and there he begins to undo the mistakes of the first.

Crossing the Kidron valley to Gethsemane after the Last Supper, Jesus enters the darkness, and he begins 'to be distressed and agitated' (Mark 14.33). The hour of his Passion is dawning. Luke tells us that 'In his anguish he prayed more earnestly, and his sweat became like great drops of blood falling down on the ground' (22.44). The Greek word translated 'anguish' (NRSV) or 'agony' (RSV) is *agonia*, and this is the only time it is used in the New Testament. It denotes a struggle for victory, a contest, a battle with physical, mental and spiritual dimensions. Gethsemane becomes a place of demons and angels locked in combat (Luke 22.43, 44). Christ's prayer in Gethsemane, in which he truly wrestles with God, and in which chalice and sword represent different and conflicting paths to take (Luke 22.42, 50), invites *us* to be prepared to struggle in prayer: to struggle with decision-making, to grapple with difficult issues, to fight with temptation. But it also invites us to move from struggle to surrender, as we cry out with Christ, 'Not my will but yours be done.' The evangelical Mother Basilea Schlink understands Gethsemane in terms of dramatic confrontation:

> Now the time had come when Jesus, who is the very essence of life, had to confront the prince of death, who had assembled all the forces of his kingdom, the entire host of evil spirits. In this crucial hour, would Jesus in his human frailty abandon the struggle as Adam and Eve once did? . . . Jesus took up Satan's challenge and entered this terrible battle with hell.[7]

Gethsemane reminds us of the place of spiritual combat in prayer. The prayer of Gethsemane invites us to be real in prayer, with no pretending, no false pleasantries, bringing to God our painful questions, our unresolved perplexities. Sometimes in prayer we need to face our 'shadow side', the darker side of our personality; our prayer will resemble Gethsemane as a place of spiritual combat and wrestling, where struggle gives way to utter surrender to the Father of love. The Psalms remind us that there is a valid place in prayer for grappling with unresolved issues and doubts.[8] They also affirm to us that there is a way through such difficulties: new faith and trust can come to the surface and new creative perspectives can emerge in the prayer of struggle.

Questions for reflection

1 The primordial garden asks: In what ways can you 'walk with God in the cool of the day'?

2 The political garden is one of contradiction and irony. How does the idea of paradox help you to live with unresolved issues?

3 The paschal garden affirms the place of struggle in spirituality. What place is there in your prayer for spiritual struggle?

4 What is your experience of moving from struggle to surrender?

5 How can you cultivate and live a sacramental approach to creation?

For further reading

Y. K. Halevi, *At the Entrance to the Garden of Eden: A Jew's Search for God with Christians and Muslims in the Holy Land* (New York: William Morrow, 2001)

A. Laytner, *Arguing with God: A Jewish Tradition* (Northvale, NJ: Jason Aronson, 1990)

A. D. Mayes, *Spirituality of Struggle: Pathways to Growth* (London: SPCK; New York: Paulist Press, 2002)

Figure 9 Raw beauty: the Judaean wilderness confronts us

9

The desert's questions
Dare I be alone with God?

The very word 'desert' may evoke in the imagination scenes of endless windswept sand dunes, perhaps a sense of desolation. In fact, as we shall see, the desert becomes a central experience in Christian spirituality, holding in itself the very secrets of prayer, a place of radical exposure to God. In this chapter, we shall encounter four deserts: the Negev, the Judaean wilderness, the desert of the early Church, and finally the desert-spaces we must open up in the spiritual landscape of our own lives. We shall first explore the significance of the desert experience in the Bible, and then see how it becomes a formative, decisive metaphor of the Christian experience of prayer in the early centuries of the Church. As we look at the Bible stories, keep in mind these two questions: What sort of things happened in the desert? Can this sort of thing happen also in the experience and journey of prayer?

The Negev desert

The first desert is the desert of Abraham and the Exodus. This flat, sandy region is found between the Mediterranean and the Dead Sea valley. Narrowing towards the south, it becomes increasingly arid and breaks into dramatic sandstone hills. Dusty brown mountains rise amid a landscape of dirt, rocks, deep canyons and mysterious craters. Hidden in these hills today are Israel's major military installations and her nuclear arsenal. The silence of this desert is shattered from time to time as bomber jets screech overhead.

Abraham was invited by God to step into this desert and so to begin an awesome adventure with God. When he was 75 years old, God said to him, 'Go from your country and your kindred and your father's house to the land that I will show you' (Gen. 12.1). Abraham was summoned to leave behind all his securities and familiar landmarks, and venture forth into the Negev desert. He became a pilgrim and a pioneer. The desert for Abraham represented a call to relinquish control over his own destiny, to step out in trust and discover a radical dependence on God alone. His faith is celebrated in the Letter to the Hebrews: 'He set out, not knowing where he was going ... living in tents ... he looked forward to the city that has foundations, whose architect and builder is God' (Heb. 11.8–10). For Abraham, the desert was a call to quit his comfort zone and to look expectantly to God.

Moses found himself in this same desert as he led the people of Israel towards freedom. After years in the desert of Sinai, the Israelites wandered in the Negev. They found the desert to be a place where they had to grapple with physical foes. It was a place of skirmishes, battles and victories. But it was also, for the Israelites, a place where they had to face the enemy within – doubt, impatience, the rebellion of their hearts. The desert was a place of grumbling and complaint, one in which God cried out to them, 'O that today you would listen to [my] voice!' (Ps. 95.7).

Why was it that, according to the biblical perspective, the Israelites' journey lasted 40 years and not 40 days? Perhaps it was because God had some important, crucial things to teach them. First, the people discovered themselves (Exod. 19.1–8). They gained a new sense of identity and purpose. They got a sense of their dignity and destiny. They realized that they were no longer slaves in God's eyes, but priests. They went from being nobodies to being God's cherished people. They discovered a sense of peoplehood and they realized that God had plans for them.

Second, they discovered the living God in a new way (Exod. 19.16–20). In the theophany and revelation of Sinai, they encountered God and his divine will, represented in the Ten Commandments. In the desert they experienced the deliverance and providence of God. The desert was, for Moses and his people, a place of life-changing discovery. In the desert, the people came to realize that God had a destiny for them, a unique vocation.

96

Elijah also found himself in the Negev. For him it was a desert of despair and burnout, where he collapsed in exhaustion after fleeing the wicked queen Jezebel (1 Kings 19). All his stresses were catching up with him, but God sent him further across the desert to the remote mountain of Horeb. There he found God in the 'sound of sheer silence'. There God ministered to his deepest wounds. There God restored him. There God gave him a new sense of direction and replaced his frantic chaos with a clear set of priorities.

The Judaean desert

The Judaean desert stretches east from the central highlands towards the fault-line scarp of the Great Rift Valley. It is a wind-swept, rocky and rugged wilderness. Mountains, cliffs and chalk hills tower above deeply incised canyons. The chiselled ravines are parchingly dry for much of the year, but in winter, rains from Jerusalem pour through them in torrents forceful enough to move great boulders, which litter the riverbed. Acacia and juniper trees cling to the cliffs, while hawks circle overhead, the goats of the Bedouins picking their way precariously over the rocks. The Judaean desert is a place of paradox: rugged grandeur, raw splendour, untameable beauty; threatening yet inviting, affirming yet disturbing, a place of life and death. It was at the edge of these very hills that the Qumran community established itself about 100 BC; later producing the Dead Sea Scrolls, they sought to model an alternative apocalyptic community awaiting the Redeemer. The desert has always attracted those on the social margin: fugitives, solitaries, outlaws, hermits . . .

As we turn to the New Testament, we discover that the gospel actually begins in this very desert of human need: 'The beginning of the good news of Jesus Christ, the Son of God. As it is written in the prophet Isaiah, "See, I am sending my messenger ahead of you, who will prepare your way; the voice of one crying out in the wilderness: 'Prepare the way of the Lord.'"' (Mark 1.1–3). John the Baptist appears and a voice echoes among the rocks and waste places: 'Turn back to God!' The desert, symbolic of humankind's emptiness, becomes the place of salvation, the place of trans-formation, through John's call to *metanoia*, repentance, to a total reorientation of human lives towards God.

Jesus thus begins his ministry in the desert. After his baptism, he is driven by the Spirit into the inner desert. He discovers it to be a place of angels and demons, as Mark succinctly puts it: 'He was in the wilderness for forty days, tempted by Satan; and he was with the wild beasts; and the angels waited on him' (Mark 1.13). Jesus experiences the desert as a place of conflict, in which he decisively battles with shortcuts to prestige, pride and power. But, most of all, it is the place where he learns to discern the Father's voice, and discovers the priorities for his ensuing ministry. Here he learns what was to become the secret of his ministry: 'Very truly, I tell you, the Son can do nothing on his own, but only what he sees his Father doing . . . The Father loves the Son and shows him all that he himself is doing' (John 5.19, 20). In his desert prayer, Jesus glimpses the divine imperatives that will guide him in the days ahead. Amid the rocks he clarifies his personal mission, and sees what is important, and what is not. Amid the rocks, Jesus comes to understand his vocation clearly: the experience crystallizes his sense of direction, his very purpose.

The desert in the early Church

When the Emperor Constantine, in 313, proclaimed religious freedom throughout the Roman Empire for Christians, everything changed for the Church: the deserts beckoned once more. And when in 380, the Emperor Theodosius declared Christianity to be the state religion throughout the whole of the empire, Christendom was born, and the call of the desert became louder and more irresistible. For after the end of the persecutions, nominalism and mediocrity crept into the Church. Now it was so easy to be a Christian; in fact, everyone was a Christian – of sorts. But to some it seemed that the standards of discipleship were being watered down, and only a superficial commitment to Christ was needed. Seeking to rediscover a radical Christianity, first tens, then hundreds, then thousands went to the desert. In search of a more challenging discipleship, they created settlements in the deserts of Egypt, Palestine, Syria and Asia Minor. The 'red martyrdom' of shedding blood was over – this was the 'white martyrdom', in which Christians sought to die to the self and allow the Risen Christ to live in them. They went into the desert to discover an authentic spirituality; whether living alone as hermits or together in community, these men and women pursued the same aim – to come face to face with God.

In the Byzantine period, the Judaean wilderness was flooded with monks seeking seclusion. The title of Derwas Chitty's book sums up the phenomenon: *The Desert a City*. At the height of the Byzantine period in the sixth century AD, there were 70 monasteries in the Judaean desert. Today one can visit seven living monasteries. In the narrow ravine of the Wadi Faran, in the desert east of Jerusalem, we find the very first Judaean monastery, founded in 275 by St Chariton. These days a sole Russian monk occupies this cave complex, the silence broken only by the babble of the nearby spring and by birdsong echoing around the sheer white cliffs. The Greek Orthodox monastic village of Mar Saba, dating from the fifth century and one of the oldest continually occupied monasteries in the world, has grown barnacle-like on the cliffs above the Kidron valley. Also near Bethlehem are the fortress-monasteries of St Theodosius and St Elias. In the depths of the Wadi Kelt a small community resides at St George of Kobiza, while clinging precariously to the precipitous cliffs above Jericho is the Monastery of the Temptation of Christ. Near the River Jordan, five miles north of the Dead Sea, lies the Greek Orthodox monastery of St Gerasimus.

There are also ruins to be discovered: one can visit substantial remnants of the monastery of St Euthymius (377–473), who established the pattern for Palestinian monasticism by insisting that those who desired the eremitical (solitary) life were first trained in cenobitic tradition (life in community). The remnants of one monastery are to be found in the scary Wadi Og. In his sixth-century account of the discovery of this site by Theoctistus and Euthymius as a suitable place of prayer and retreat, Cyril of Scythopolis gives us a vivid sense of the topography:

As they passed through the desert they came to a terrifying gorge, extremely steep and impassable. On seeing the place and going round the cliffs above it they found, as if guided by God, a huge and marvellous cave in the northern cliff of the gorge. Not without danger they made the steep ascent and just managed to climb up to it. Overjoyed as if the cave had been prepared for them by God, they made it their home.[1]

The desert of discipleship

Basil of Caesarea (330–379) played a vital role in helping to bring the vision of desert monasticism to the wider world. He visited the monastic settlements of Palestine, Syria and Egypt in order to discover their secret. On his return to Cappadocia he embodied his insights in his Rule, which to this day is central to Eastern monasticism, while Benedict acknowledged his debt to Basil in his own Rule, which became the basis of Western monasticism. In his letter to his friend Gregory Nazianzus, written to persuade him to come and join the retreat at Pontus, Basil explores four aspects of the call of the desert.[2]

First, the desert calls us to stillness and silence. Basil writes: 'One should aspire at keeping the mind in quietude [*hesychia*].' The Desert Fathers echo this theme. The story is told:

Abba Macarius the Great said to the brothers at Scetis, when he dismissed the assembly, 'Flee, my brothers.' One of the old men asked him, 'Where could we flee to beyond this desert?' He put his finger on his lips and said, 'Flee that,' and he went into his cell, shut the door and sat down.[3]

Second, the desert calls us to solitude. Basil explains: 'The solitude [*eremia*] offers a very great advantage for our task of prayer. Let us for a season be free from the commerce of men, so that nothing may come from without and break the continuity of the *ascesis* [training or discipline].' There is a place in discipleship for getting off the treadmill of work and activity, saying goodbye to the clamour of things in the world that forever compete for our attention, in order, for a while at least, that we may become focused on God and utterly attentive to him.

Third, the desert calls us to detachment. Basil writes: 'Now this withdrawal [*anachoresis*, retreat] does not mean that we should leave the world bodily, but rather break loose from the ties of "sympathy" of the soul with the body.' Basil is extolling the virtues of making a retreat from activity, for a few minutes, or hours, or days. He says that, for a season, we have to cut our ties, loosen our grip and grasp on activities, let go of our attachments and our worries. This is so we can become wholly available to God in prayer.

Fourth, the desert calls us to receptivity. The most important thing, says Basil, is that we are 'making ready to receive in our heart the imprint of divine teaching . . . beautiful is the prayer that impresses into the mind a clear notion of God.' For Basil and the Desert Fathers and Mothers, the overriding aim is to learn to listen out for the whisper of God's voice and to discern his will and guidance.

Modern writers point out that at the heart of the experience of the Desert Fathers was the quest for inner and outer transformation. As Thomas Merton puts it:

> What the Fathers sought most of all was their own true self, in Christ. And in order to do this, they had to reject completely the false, formal self, fabricated under social compulsion in 'the world.' . . . A life of solitude and labour, poverty and fasting, charity and prayer which enabled the old superficial self to be purged away and permitted the gradual emergence of the true, secret self in which the Believer and Christ were 'one Spirit.'[4]

Henri Nouwen echoes this view:

> Solitude is not a private therapeutic place. Rather, it is the place of conversion, the place where the old self dies and the new self is born . . . Solitude is the place where Christ remodels us in his own image and frees us from the victimizing compulsions of the world. Solitude is the place of our salvation.[5]

Questions from the desert

The physical desert, into which the heroes of the Old Testament ventured, and which was so vital to Jesus and the early Church, poses crucial questions to us today.

Dare you open up a space for God in your life?

The physical desert is a place of exposure to sun and wind, where there is nowhere to hide. It calls us to seek a spiritual state or condition in which we become naked before God, exposing heart and mind to the wind of his Spirit and the warmth of his love. The desert is a place of persistent erosion, where wind and even water wear down the resistance of stubborn rocks and refashion their shapes. There are unremitting processes of disintegration at work in the desert landscape, as well as processes of formation and building up. So, too, in prayer we must learn to become susceptible to God and open to his ever-creative remoulding. In prayer, our normal guard needs to melt away so that God is allowed to reshape our life and our priorities. As there is an immediacy in the desert, where all props are gone and only essential things matter, so in prayer masks drop off. In prayer we risk facing up in utter honesty to the realities of our lives. As Jerome put it, from his fourth-century monastery at Bethlehem: 'The desert loves to strip bare.'[6]

Dare you thirst for more of God in prayer?

The desert speaks powerfully of our spiritual poverty. It reminds us to confront the aridity of our lives, and to recognize where there might be signs of emptiness. As Macarius wrote: 'We have an insatiable longing for the Spirit, to shine out – the more spiritual gifts we enjoy, the more insatiable is the heavenly desire in our hearts, the more hungry and thirsty we are for more grace.'[7] Thus the desert of prayer becomes a place of deep renewal and experience of the Holy Spirit. Isaiah the prophet sees the desert as a symbol of humanity's need – a natural analogy for our need of God. The desert represents spiritual poverty and human thirst for the divine:

For I will pour water on the thirsty land,
and streams on the dry ground;
I will pour my Spirit upon your descendants,
and my blessing on your offspring.
(Isa. 44.3; cf. 35.1–10; 41.17–20)

Dare you embrace prayer itself as pilgrimage and exploration?

We have seen how in Scripture the desert was a place of pilgrimage and discovery. This invites us to consider the experience of prayer itself as a terrain to be explored, a place of mystery in which we can find out new things about ourselves and about God. Prayer is a quest or search in the holy space which spans ultimacy and intimacy, the discovery of God as Source and as *Abba*. Silences can open up for us desert-like spaces where we find ourselves to be learners of God. The desert rouses us to explore more deeply the mystery of God and the mystery of our self. It attests that we are called to be explorers of the inner space.

Dare you break the silence?

As Ecclesiastes reminds us, there is 'a time to keep silence, and a time to speak' (Eccles. 3.7). If in the silence we clarify our priorities as did Jesus and listen for the Father's voice, we are also being equipped for those times when we need to break the silence. While today a deep silence lingers amid the rocks of the Judaean desert, sometimes conflicting sounds can be heard: howling winds funnelled down the gullies; the timeless flute and call of the Bedouin shepherd-boy as he minds flocks of goats and sheep. The night air is pierced by the wailing of jackals and the laughter of hyenas, while by day the jarring, hammering sound of rock-breaking machinery and earth-moving equipment arises from construction sites, where new Jewish settlements turn the desert, once again, into a city. This reminds us: there are times when a silence *should* be ended. There are times when we need the courage and passion of John the Baptist to be 'a voice in the wilderness' and speak out a prophetic word of encouragement or critique in relation to society around us.

Questions for reflection

1 What is your experience of solitude?
2 Basil writes: '*Askesis* nurtures the soul with divine thoughts.' The word *askesis* means literally training or exercise. It evokes Paul's picture of a spiritual athlete (1 Cor. 9.24–27). What forms of spiritual training do you need to develop? And if being a disciple entails disciplines, what place is there today for spiritual disciplines?
3 How helpful do you find the description of prayer as 'a terrain to be explored'?
4 Can you identify any ways in which you sense you should 'break the silence' – where a prophetic word of critique or encouragement needs to be spoken out?
5 To what extent do you find the desert a positive image of spirituality?
6 How far do you find that physical landscapes mirror the interior life of the human spirit?

For further reading

D. Chitty, *The Desert a City: An Introduction to the Study of Egyptian and Palestinian Monasticism Under the Christian Empire* (New York: St Vladimir's Seminary Press, 1997)

B. C. Lane, *The Solace of Fierce Landscapes* (Oxford: Oxford University Press, 1998)

H. Nouwen, *The Way of the Heart: Desert Spirituality and Contemporary Ministry* (London: Darton, Longman & Todd, 1987)

B. Ward, *The Wisdom of the Desert Fathers* (Oxford: SLG Press, 1986)

Figure 10 Walls in pieces: Titus' destruction of Temple buildings

10

The wall's questions

What is stopping me?

The landscape of the Holy Land is marked by some stunning natural walls. The precipitous cliffs that form the escarpment west of the River Jordan and the Dead Sea denote the edge of the plateau of the central highlands and the border of the Judaean wilderness. In the Negev desert, the sheer walls that drop 2,000 feet below Mitzpe Ramon form the side of a spectacular crater 25 miles long. These Grand Canyon-like walls reveal coloured and contrasting strata that tell the story of the earth's formation through millions of years. And all across the land, there are man-made walls, each with a story to tell: walls to be admired and walls to be feared. The visitor to Jerusalem encounters three major walls.

First are the sixteenth-century crenellated battlements encircling the city, built by Suleiman the Magnificent, white stone aglow in the sunshine: they can be explored by a walk on the ramparts. The walls of Jerusalem, originating in the fear of attack and the imperative to close the community off protectively, have been destroyed and rebuilt 18 times throughout history. A Jebusite wall, revealed by archaeology, testifies to Jerusalem's early history: David encountered this in his initial attack in about 1000 BC (2 Sam. 5). Three hundred years later, Hezekiah strengthened the city's defences in the face of the Assyrian threat: his massive Broad Wall, 8 metres high and 8 metres thick, has come to the light of day, once again, in recent excavations in the Jewish quarter. Nehemiah's mission in the sixth century BC was to rebuild the walls after their destruction by the Babylonians, and he gives us a vivid account (Neh. 4—6). In AD 70 the Romans besieged the city, which had come under the control of Jewish zealots. Titus' forces used battering rams and siege towers in an attempt to destroy the fortifications, but it was fire that brought the walls around the Temple crashing down.

The Tenth Legion was headquartered in the Citadel. Hadrian rebuilt the walls when remodelling the city as Aelia Capitolina in AD 135, and his forum is still to be seen beneath Damascus Gate. The walls have since seen a succession of attacks: by the Crusaders in 1099 and Saladin in 1187; by General Allenby, who initiated the British Mandate in 1921 by claiming control of the bulwarks; and, after bitter fighting in June 1967, by Israeli snipers who scaled the parapets to seize charge of them.

The second wall which the pilgrim is likely to see came to new life in 1967, for the conquering soldiers' first priority was to open up access to the Western Wall, the retaining wall of the Second Temple, as a place of prayer for Jewish people. For the Jewish pilgrim, touching the Western Wall is a tangible link and connection to the destroyed Temple: it is also called the Wailing Wall, for here Jews lament the destruction of their sanctuary. As the Western Wall Foundation's visitors' leaflet puts it: 'The Western Wall has been the centre of Jewish yearning and memory for more than 2000 years . . . The Wall has withstood time, it has witnessed war and peace, destruction and revival. For generations, it has absorbed the prayers and yearnings of those near and far.' After passing through the security checkpoint, where bags and bodies are scanned, one may approach the wall itself: into its cracks Jewish pilgrims press folded papers bearing their prayers, and before the wall young men dance at a Bar Mitzvah ceremony and old men sob at the memory of the Temple's demise. Before this wall, in their 'passing out' ceremony, young conscripts to the Israeli Defence Forces pledge their oath of loyalty to the State.

A third wall to be encountered, known as '*The* Wall', the Separation Barrier, has been erected on grounds of security, ostensibly to prevent Palestinian suicide bombers crossing into Israel proper. It consists in places of concrete slabs 30 feet tall; elsewhere it is an electrified fence reinforced with sophisticated surveillance equipment and razor wire. It has been called an apartheid barrier, but it not only separates Arab from Jew but often also slices Arab neighbourhoods in half, preventing farmers from reaching their fields or grandmothers seeing their grandchildren. The Wall has had the effect of cutting off the West Bank territories from Jerusalem, and it bitterly restricts the travel options of Palestinian West Bankers. Workers may have to queue for hours each morning at the checkpoints manned by the Israeli Defence Forces, and special permissions are required to visit the holy places at time of festivals. Only with immense difficulty can men over 50 years of age worship in Jerusalem, whether at the Muslim Al Aqsa Mosque or the Christian Church of the Resurrection: men under 50 are regularly prohibited altogether. A UN report states: 'It is difficult to overestimate the humanitarian impact of the Barrier. The route inside the West Bank severs communities, people's access to services, livelihoods and religious and cultural amenities.'[1] The Wall has developed a stranglehold on the people of the West Bank, and is experienced as oppressively dominating ordinary lives.

These three major walls are physical barriers that pilgrims can see with their own eyes. In addition there are invisible but no less palpable walls within and across communities – walls of suspicion and misunderstanding, walls of fear and prejudice. The common feature of the walls is that they represent defensiveness, possessiveness; they separate people and reinforce divides. Walls can denote a narrowing of vision.

Breaking down the walls

But in Jerusalem and in the Holy Land, walls have come tumbling down. We think of the account of the collapsing walls of Jericho (Josh. 6). Most traces of the walls of the ancient City of David have largely disappeared beneath the Arab village of Silwan; there are just a few remnants to be seen of Agrippa's mighty Third Wall built in AD 44 north of the city. And even today there are places that breach walls and make access possible. There are seven great city gates that bid one to cross the threshold into a different world, opening up the wonder of exploring the different quarters of the Holy City: a stunning flight of steps descends to the magnificent

Damascus Gate, its inspiring Ottoman architecture leading into the northern city; the wide and noble Jaffa Gate opens the city to the west. The 'Gate of Mercy' and 'Gate of Repentance' comprise the Golden Gate on the eastern side of the Temple Mount – but these are blocked and await, according to tradition, the returning Messiah to open them. In Bethlehem the 'Door of Humility' marks the entrance into the Basilica of the Nativity. On the Gaza Strip people even dig risky tunnels in the sand under the border fence with Egypt in order to open up a passage for goods and travellers. There are a variety of ways that walls can be overcome.

Psalm 18.29 invites us to dismantle walls: 'By you I can crush a troop, and by my God I can leap over a wall.' The most urgent need in Jerusalem today is for barriers to be opened up – so that they become doors of understanding, windows of perception, and provide opportunities for listening between local Christians, Muslims and Jews. We need the courage to cross new thresholds of understanding, and to help dismantle walls of misunderstanding where they exist.

This requires pilgrims to examine their *own* walls. It demands of pilgrims a readiness to lower the self-protective barriers that we unconsciously erect around ourselves to protect ourselves from getting too close to what might challenge us. We need the grace to first recognize, then chip away at, our own walls and defences. This is a basic requirement for pilgrims – to be ready for some measure of brokenness and honesty, as we expose our hearts and minds to new insights, new ways of seeing things, different cultures. This is the essential risk of learning – to be willing to change!

But the dismantling of walls requires both human effort and divine grace. We must not only be prepared for hard work in changing our attitudes, we must open ourselves afresh to the grace of Christ. He is the one who breaks down walls and opens up new possibilities. He is the one who makes breakthroughs possible. He calls himself 'the gate' (John 10.9). At the start of his ministry and at the end of it, what was formerly closed is now opened up. At his baptism he sees the walls of heaven itself torn apart (Mark 1.10). At his death the heavy curtain separating the Temple's Holy of Holies from the people, a persistent barrier between humans and God, is likewise torn apart, from top to bottom (Mark 15.38). On Easter Day, when the disciples hide themselves away and the doors are 'locked for fear', the Risen Christ is not impeded by walls of anxiety: he breaks through and greets his people with the words: 'Peace be with you' (John 20.19). As the Letter to the Ephesians puts it: 'He . . . has broken down the dividing wall, that is, the hostility between us . . . through the cross' (Eph. 2.14, 16).

Studies in cultural anthropology help us to understand Christ's dismantling of walls against the background of the dynamics and mindsets prevailing in first-century society, especially the status/ shame divide.[2] In the society of Jesus' time, people were kept apart by a sense of hierarchy, in which honour was ascribed to patriarchal families and to the well-to-do, while at the opposite end of the spectrum, shame was associated with the social nobodies: not only obvious social outcasts like tax collectors (deemed to be collaborators with the Romans) and prostitutes, but also children and women. The Gospels are full of episodes in which Jesus crosses boundaries and breaks down barriers. For him the child in the midst is the model of true greatness (Mark 9.33–37). The presence of women is welcomed by Jesus (Luke 8.3; 23.49) and Mary Magdalene is the first witness of the resurrection. Jesus reaches out to those marginalized by society, embracing the leper (Luke 17.12–19). In Jerusalem, as he throws down the tables of the money-changers in the Temple, he welcomes the outcasts and the ritually unclean: 'The blind and the lame came to him in the temple, and he cured them' (Matt. 21.14). The most significant sign of his inclusive kingdom, where barriers are overturned, is the meal where Jesus eats with tax collectors and sinners (Luke 5.29–32; see also Luke 14.12–24). For Jesus, the open table – where everyone, regardless of shame or status, has an honoured place – expresses his readiness to smash barriers and social taboos. This has led scholars to think of Jesus not only as a social revolutionary, but also as a social prophet, embodying his message in cutting word and symbolic action.[3] Certainly, Jesus emerges in the Gospels as a wall-breaker. Looking at the mighty walls of Jerusalem, Jesus foresees their demolition: 'You're impressed by this grandiose architecture? There's not a stone in the whole works that is not going to end up in a heap of rubble' (Mark 13.2, *The Message*).

The example of St Francis

In a story strongly linked with the Holy Land, we hear of how St Francis of Assisi exemplified this Christlike spirit in courageously crossing impossible-looking barriers. In 1219, during the Fifth Crusade, the Christian knights were besieging the city of Damietta on the Nile, an important entry point for pilgrims travelling towards the Holy Land. The Crusaders' mission was to open up the routes of pilgrimage to the Church of the Resurrection, which were in Muslim hands. Their strategy, of course, was the way of violence: they aimed to slaughter as many followers of Islam as they could. When Francis arrived in Damietta, he tried to dissuade the Crusaders from their bloody action, but nobody listened. So, accompanied by one brother, Illuminato, Francis crossed the battle lines. First he left the relative safety of the Crusader military camp. Francis had to step into the no-man's-land which separated the warring factions and, in order to reach the enemy camp, had to traverse forbidding defensive ditches and heavily armed enemy barriers. On reaching the city of Damietta, he fearlessly crossed three walls. His aim was to reach the Sultan of Egypt himself, Malek al Kamil, nephew of Saladin the Great who had taken Jerusalem in 1187.

He was turned back at every point, but was resolute and, having somehow got past the soldiers guarding the walls that kept the two camps apart, he succeeded in holding an extended dialogue with the Sultan, who received him with deep respect. For his part, Francis saw the Sultan as a brother, and in the process learned a great deal about the foreign world of Islam, glimpsing new perspectives on 'the infidel religion' which had been viewed in the West through the eyes of prejudice and fear. Francis was changed by this meeting, and it left an abiding mark on his own spirituality. The litany on the divine names, *The Praises of God*, which he composed later, after receiving the stigmata at Mount La Verna, looks like a meditation on the Islamic Ninety-nine Names of God:

'You are holy, Lord, the only God . . . You are strong, you are great, you are the Most High, you are almighty . . . You are Good, all Good, supreme Good.'

In his deeds at Damietta, Francis emerges as an intrepid and audacious risk-taker, energized by the love of Christ, as he breaches the walls dividing two peoples. His encounter with the Sultan is sometimes considered to be the first example of genuine Christian–Muslim dialogue. Certainly it has inspired many to realize how walls can be breached. It is understood that Francis later made it to the Holy Land itself, and the presence of Franciscans here was to achieve by peaceful means what the Crusaders had sought to gain through violence and brutality: to this day the Franciscans open up access to the holy places.

Chipping away at the walls

Brick by brick, as it were, walls of division are being dismantled in Jerusalem today. One often hears in the city the sound of hammer against stone, as if people are chipping away at the walls.

- *A courageous dialogue between faiths,* involving patient listening in an effort to deepen mutual understanding, is exemplified by the interfaith ministry of the Anglican Diocese of Jerusalem, the work of the Sisters of Our Lady of Zion (Ratisbonne Sisters), and Jewish and Muslim initiatives like the Interreligious Coordinating Council in Israel.
- *A growing sense of unity between Christians* reveals itself in the high level of cooperation between the heads of the 13 historic churches of Jerusalem, who have regular meetings and prayer together, and in small, hidden communities of prayer and study like the Sisters of St Elizabeth at Even Sapir, the Beatitudes Community at Emmaus, and the Ecumenical Theological Research Fraternity. Diverse Christians from overseas are working together in the World Council of Churches project entitled the Ecumenical Accompaniment Program in Palestine and Israel (EAPPI), and in Christian Peacemaker teams involved in violence reduction.

- *The compassion of the Risen Christ towards the hurting* is manifested at every hand in projects like the Princess Basma Centre for Disabled Children, the Anglican Gaza and Nablus hospitals, the Spafford Centre . . . which see every day untold acts of generosity and selflessness.
- *Teaching programmes and pilgrimages*, enabling real encounters with the living stones of local Christians, are expanding at places of learning and prayer like St George's College, Tantur Ecumenical Institute, and the Sabeel centre for liberation theology.
- *Reconciliation among youth* is taking place in small-scale projects which bring Arab and Jewish young people together in mutual respect and fun, like kids4peace (run by the Episcopal Diocese of Jerusalem) and the Seeds of Peace. Churches operate an impressive array of schools, releasing the potential, laughter and hopefulness of children. Some churches (for example, Ramallah's Anglican parish) sponsor vocational training schemes for youth, aiming to strengthen their confidence and to encourage them to stay in the country.
- Most impressive of all, perhaps, is the *faithfulness of ordinary people*, expressed by the Palestinian concept of *samud*: stickability, endurance and resilience under testing circumstances, despite discouragement and fatigue. This is more than resignation in the face of difficult circumstances: it is living in sometimes dehumanizing situations with dignity and a sense of purpose.

So Jerusalem – the Holy City – is a place of walls, but also a place where breakthroughs occur, where Christ waits to lead us across boundaries and through barriers, to new places of encounter. The walls challenge us to discover how defences can be dismantled. They challenge us to open up new doors of perception into Scripture and new ways of understanding discipleship and ministry. And just as the city gates – as their names suggest – not only lead pilgrims in but also send them out (Jaffa Gate leading to the coast and Damascus Gate towards the north), so may our discoveries in Jerusalem and in our own land lead us out into more courageous mission.

Questions for reflection

1 How can you identify your own self-protective fences?
2 How prepared are you to lower your defences as you encounter the Other?
3 In what ways are you being called to dismantle fences and become a reconciler?
4 How can you support the efforts in the Middle East to remove barriers of hatred?
5 What is stopping you or holding you back from becoming the person God wants you to be?

For further reading

P. Moses, *The Saint and the Sultan: The Crusades, Islam and Francis of Assisi's Mission of Peace* (New York: Doubleday Religion, 2001)

C. Westerhoff, *Good Fences: The Boundaries of Hospitality* (Cambridge, MA: Cowley Publications, 1999)

Figure 11 Risky path: the Emmaus Road at Moza

11

The road's questions

Am I ready for change?

———•◆•———

'Thus says the LORD: Stand at the crossroads, and look, and ask for the ancient paths, where the good way lies; and walk in it, and find rest for your souls' (Jer. 6.16). The pilgrim to the Holy Land becomes aware of these ancient paths traversing ridge and valley, their stones full of biblical memories, evocative of the travels of ancestors in the faith and of Jesus himself. The visitor also notices the massive road-building works in progress today. The terrain is becoming scarred by new highways which are reshaping the topography, sometimes with a devastating effect on the environment. While the traditional paths clung to the contours of the landscape, following old stone walls along the terraces or dry valley-bottoms, these new roads are often dynamited through hillsides and require tunnels beneath the mountains.

Ancient pathways

The hillsides are criss-crossed by many tracks, which if they could speak, would have a multitude of stories to tell: Canaanites on their way to market or to family weddings in neighbouring villages; Israelites establishing a presence in the land through Joshua's settlements ... In the hills of Judaea the Way of the Patriarchs, leading south from Jerusalem to Hebron, can be traced to this period; the route was used more than three millennia ago by the caravans of Abraham, Isaac and Jacob. This same road has been used by pilgrims to the Holy City through the centuries. The Romans developed and strengthened the road in their characteristic fashion, and their old kerbstones and milestones are still to be found.

The three major north–south roads that existed in the time of Jesus are still in use today. The Via Maris, the Way of the Sea, is referred to in the famous prophecy: 'There will be no gloom for those who were in anguish . . . in the latter time he will make glorious the way of the sea, the land beyond the Jordan, Galilee of the nations' (Isa. 9.1). This ancient trade route between Egypt and Mesopotamia is in long stretches followed to this day by the modern Route 6 toll-road.

The second major road of Jesus' time is the route through Samaria. This road was especially significant for Jesus, passing as it did through the hostile lands of the Samaritans. 'Jews do not share things in common with Samaritans' (John 4.9), but this road was intentionally taken by Jesus on his pilgrimage journeys from Galilee to Jerusalem. This road is rarely suitable for Christian pilgrimages today, for it encounters many checkpoints as it traverses the West Bank; part of it follows the northern section of the Way of the Patriarchs, from Shechem to Jerusalem, via the ancient sanctuaries of Bethel and Shiloh.

Third, the ancient Jordan valley road remains a major route, passing today the electrified wire fences that mark the border with the state of Jordan. It approaches Jericho via the Valley of Achor, which Hosea called 'a door of hope' (2.15). After Jericho the traveller to Jerusalem turns west: here the road climbs steeply, from over 800 feet below sea level to an altitude of 2,600 feet at the Mount of Olives, reminding us that the Jewish word for pilgrimage is *aliyah*, meaning 'to go up' (as we saw in Chapter 1, this word is also used to denote the return of Jews to the land): 'Let us go to the house of the LORD!' (Ps. 122). The Psalms of Ascent (Pss. 120—134) cheered pilgrims on their tough upward trek through the wilderness of Judaea between Jerusalem and the Jordan; the ambush in the parable of the Good Samaritan (Luke 10.25–37) reminds us how dangerous this road could be. Indeed it could be the 'valley of the shadow of death' of the twenty-third Psalm, which discovers God's shepherd-like care in the midst of a dangerous route.

Modern highways

Today this once narrow and treacherous road, weaving its way through the mountains, is being dramatically widened: broad dual carriageways have replaced the winding Roman road. Everywhere heavy machinery – excavators, earthmovers and bulldozers – is transforming the landscape, in places damaging natural habitats and threatening ecosystems. Construction of highways goes hand-in-hand with the destruction and concretization of the terrain. It is a sign of Israel's resolve to establish and control the transport network before any peace process makes this impossible. No more clearly is this seen than on the West Bank, where an entire parallel network of Israeli settler-only roads, prohibited to Palestinians, creates an infrastructure to serve the multiplying Jewish settlements. These brand-new bypass roads carve their way through the landscape, while older roads, left for the Arabs, fall into decay and are marked with military checkpoints at regular intervals or with what are called 'internal closures'. Traditional routes into Jerusalem have been barred by the Separation Barrier.

Biblical metaphors

Biblical writers utilize the image of the pathway or road as a metaphor for entering upon God's way of justice and salvation. Psalm 24 prays for guidance:

> Make me to know your ways, O LORD;
> teach me your paths . . .
> He leads the humble in what is right,
> and teaches the humble his way.
> All the paths of the LORD are steadfast love and
> faithfulness.   (Ps. 25.4, 9, 10a)

The prophet Isaiah envisions a path to redemption: 'A highway shall be there, and it shall be called the Holy Way; the unclean shall not travel on it, but it shall be for God's people; no traveller, not even fools, shall go astray . . . but the redeemed shall walk there. And the ransomed of the LORD shall return, and come to

Zion with singing' (35.8–10). The prophet hopes for the people's return from their exile, and sees the bleak desert becoming a 'road of holiness' and a new exodus journey towards freedom. This imagery is echoed in the vision that is taken up by John the Baptist:

> He went into all the region around the Jordan, proclaiming a baptism of repentance for the forgiveness of sins, as it is written in the book of the words of the prophet Isaiah, 'The voice of one crying out in the wilderness: "Prepare the way of the Lord, make his paths straight. Every valley shall be filled, and every mountain and hill shall be made low, and the crooked shall be made straight, and the rough ways made smooth; and all flesh shall see the salvation of God."'
>
> (Luke 3.3–6; cf. John 1.23)

John identifies closely with the landscape. As he looks out on the wild and precipitous cliffs and escarpments of the Judaean wilderness, he can envision with Isaiah a levelling of the impossible natural barriers and the raising of new pathways to freedom. What was impassable and impenetrable becomes a gateway to a new future for God's people. John's message is that we need to open up in the landscape of our lives entry points for the coming Messiah.

Roads of conversion

In Scripture, the road is the place of encounter and conversion, the place of surprise, where the traveller must be open to unexpected happenings and people. While the mountains may represent strength and the ability to dominate landscape, embodied in the hilltop stronghold, the valleys are places of vulnerability and exposure. Many roads follow the valleys, but here travellers are prey to surprise attack: in the Old Testament Gideon's forces swoop down on the Midianite troops in the Jezreel valley (Judg. 7.12–23) and the Philistines threaten David and his people in the valley of Elah (1 Samuel 17.1–2, 19). The Arameans, sensing victory, jibe to the Israelites: 'The LORD is a god of the hills but he is not a god of the valleys' (1 Kings 20.28). Unsuspecting travellers are attacked by marauding bandits. On the road, something good or bad can happen, and no one can foretell. A major theme in Mark's Gospel is the disciples' following Jesus along an unpredictable road: 'They were on the road, going up to Jerusalem, and Jesus was walking ahead of them; they were amazed' (Mark 10.32).

In John's Gospel, the Samaritan woman, coming to draw water from Jacob's well, an important stopping place on the road through Samaria, does not expect to see a Jewish traveller sitting by the well in the noonday heat. She is not expecting him to ask her for a drink, or to turn out to be 'a man who told me everything I have ever done!' (John 4.29). For the Samaritan woman, this was a life-changing encounter with a Stranger. So, too, the Ethiopian pilgrim, travelling on the road from Jerusalem to Gaza, has not bargained on Philip to draw alongside him and to open to him the meaning of an enigmatic passage of Scripture (Acts 8.26–40). This encounter leads him into new faith in Jesus, sealed by baptism in waters beside the road. Saul truly finds the road to Damascus to be a place of conversion as he encounters the Risen Christ in a vision, when he is least expecting it (Acts 9.1–19): for him, Jesus was a dead man. Yet his encounter leads to a life-shattering experience, and an utterly new direction as he discovers a commission to be 'apostle to the Gentiles'.

Likewise, today, the traveller in the Holy Land must be prepared for the unpredictable and for the potential for conversion. There are hazards which cannot be foreseen: the erection of a new military checkpoint, the closure of a road. There are unexpected natural dangers: torrential flash floods can sweep across the main road beside the Dead Sea when there is a downpour in Jerusalem, the floods gaining momentum as they course through the narrow wadis or ravines of the Judaean wilderness. There can be unexpected wildlife on the roads: camels, ibex or gazelles suddenly impeding the flow of traffic, or, overhead, the wondrous sight of flocks of migrating birds, large numbers of which make their passage from Europe to Africa over Israel.

The roads in the Holy Land often open up the traveller to astonishing and breathtaking new vistas: as when the road through the Judaean wilderness leads to a dramatic change of scenery upon reaching the wide Jordan rift valley, the mountains of Gilead and Moab rising majestically beyond the river, the stunning green oasis of Jericho promising refreshment after the desert. There can be unexpected glimpses of human settlements: new Israeli construction sites springing up, as it seems overnight, or the shanty-town tents of the Bedouin, sheep and goats herded nearby. Such experiences sometimes come 'out of the blue' for the pilgrim, and require what liberation theologians call 'conversion to the neighbour'; a new awareness of the plight of the oppressed, a readiness to confront pre-existing prejudices or perceptions.[1] Preparing to walk the Way of the Cross early one morning in Jerusalem, one pilgrim asked me: 'What can we expect?' I did not know how to answer. In the event, we saw on the Via Dolorosa armed soldiers, howling hungry cats, a homeless person asleep under a blanket, children skipping to school, a road-sweeper patiently gathering the dust and debris of the street. Each encounter had its own message and offered its own challenge. Our God is a God of surprises.

The road to Emmaus

Such is the message of the road to Emmaus: it is a place of surprising encounter, yesterday and today. Cleopas and his companion, as they walk this way downcast and depressed, find their hearts burning within them as they discover the Risen Christ (Luke 24.32). From the direction of Jerusalem, an evocative Roman road in the pineclad Sorek valley leads to Moza, which scholars now favour as the most likely location for Luke's story. It is called Ammaous by Josephus in his *Jewish War*, and later it becomes known as Colonia after veterans of the Roman army establish a colony there. Archaeologists have located Herodian structures, bespeaking a leafy suburb of Jerusalem, and Byzantine and Crusader remains.[2] Nearby lies today's 'road into the future' – the highway which modern travellers must take on their way from the holy city to the airport at the conclusion of a pilgrimage: the noisy motorway, with its traffic roaring through the narrow gorge, is juxtaposed with the silence of the adjoining valley served by the ancient road. Indeed, the modern highway, mentioned at the start of Chapter 5 as the scene of bitter fighting in 1948, follows the ancient trade route between Jerusalem and the Mediterranean ports.

As pilgrims walk on remnants of Roman pavements near Moza, in a gorge cut into 300-foot limestone cliffs, the road itself becomes a parable about encountering the Risen Christ. Four things strike the pilgrim-walker. First, this road to Emmaus is a risky place to walk. The valley is exposed, and the road is eroded and hazardous. Its surface is uneven, and one can stumble over broken stones. This is not the experience of a comfortable afternoon stroll, but rather one of facing risk and vulnerability. It is precisely here that the Risen Christ waits to meet the traveller. Sometimes the deep peace of the road is shattered by unnerving volleys from a nearby firing range, where young soldiers are trained in target practice, the sound ricocheting through the tranquil valley. Sometimes helicopters swoop deafeningly overhead. Yes, the road to Emmaus here feels risky.

Second, the walker needs to have a wakeful alertness; one must literally watch one's step. But, like Cleopas, one should not be looking down all the time, eyes to the ground. Not only would the walker miss the natural beauty of the gorge, with its fragrant conifers, but she might also miss the presence of an Other, the Stranger who draws close. This is a call to walk the road as contemplatives in movement; to contemplate is literally to 'look attentively'. Cleopas was given the gift of eyes that were opened (Luke 24.31).

A third lesson to be learned from the road to Emmaus, as it is experienced near Moza, concerns Christian community. Here pilgrims must help one another on the road, giving each other a hand, especially where they need to climb up on to the Roman kerb, or step over an obstacle in the path. Finally, the road needs these days to be cleared as one walks – the pathway is strewn with fallen branches and rocks over which one might trip. We need to clear a pathway, and remove from it the detritus and occasional garbage. The path needs to be decluttered: as one walks, one must remove impediments in order to progress in the journey. There are many things to be learned in the Holy Land from the roads, which speak to our ongoing spiritual journey. A contrast may be drawn between tourists and pilgrims: the word tourist, coming from the Old French word for 'tower', suggests that the traveller sees things from a safe, uninvolved distance; the word pilgrim derives from the Latin *per agri*, meaning 'beyond the fields', suggesting the image of one who is prepared to take a risky road, less well known. Which will we be?

There is another possible site for Emmaus: the liturgical Emmaus at Qubeibeh, where hundreds of Christian pilgrims come for the Franciscans' Easter Monday Eucharist. But normally, today, this road to Emmaus is blocked. Only courageous pilgrims will attempt this path, with the delay and humiliation of its military checkpoints. While the site is seven miles from Jerusalem, as in Luke's account (24.13), one must travel a circuitous route of 20 miles in order to reach it, due to road closures. This road to Emmaus goes through dark, unlit underpasses beneath the settlers' bypass roads and in places it is hemmed in, to right and left, by the towering walls of the Separation Barrier. But it is worth the trouble, as the topography holds more clues for our understanding. On arrival at Emmaus, 'he walked ahead as if he were going on' (Luke 24.28). Where was he bound? From this Emmaus you can taste the sea: beyond the ancient, terraced rocky hillsides lies the coastal plain, and from the church which marks the house of Cleopas and the Roman road beside it, one can glimpse the port of Jaffa in the shimmering distance, and the Mediterranean itself. You can feel the cooling sea breezes in your face. It is the sea that now summons us.

Questions for reflection

1 What is your experience of encountering the unexpected on your spiritual journey? Did this lead you to conversion or to change?

2 In the book of Isaiah, God says, 'Remove every obstruction from my people's way' (57.14) and, 'Build up the highway, clear

it of stones' (62.10). What impediments to your spiritual progress can you name? What roadblocks do you need to overcome if you are to advance in your spiritual journey?

3 Can you identify any ways in which you are becoming sidetracked or tempted to 'go off at a tangent' from your spiritual path?

4 What does Isaiah 40.3–5 look like in your own situation? How can you open up a highway for God in your community? What entry points can you recognize for evangelism? What part can you play in helping to create pathways in the desert?

5 The presence of roadblocks in the occupied territories of the Holy Land raises questions about fundamental rights to freedom of travel and human dignity. How aware are you of ways in which people in your own context are prevented or held back from achieving their true potential? What blocks people's movement towards discovering their self-worth and achieving fulfilment?

For further reading

E. Best, *Following Jesus: Discipleship in the Gospel of Mark* (Sheffield: JSOT Press, 1981)

G. W. Hughes, *Walk to Jerusalem* (London: Darton, Longman & Todd, 1991)

R. Shedadeh, *Palestinian Walks: Notes on a Vanishing Landscape* (London: Profile Books, 2007)

Figure 12 Horizons beckon: the Mediterranean at Caesarea Maritima

12

The sea's questions

What is my mission?

———••◆••———

Crashing waves from the Mediterranean Sea wash the sandy coast of this land for 117 miles. The shoreline between Lebanon and Egypt is marked by places of deepest sorrow, hedonistic pleasure and intense commerce. The sorrow: the Gaza Strip, only 25 miles long and, at most, 7 miles wide, into which are crammed 1.5 million Palestinians. It was called by British Prime Minister David Cameron 'a prison camp'.[1] Due to the persisting blockade, no ship can embark or disembark from Gaza – its coastline, sealed by the Israeli navy, does not admit even an aid flotilla. The pleasure: just a few miles north, sun-worshippers laze on the beaches and party the night away in the throbbing clubs of Tel Aviv. The commerce: the busy shipping seaport of Haifa, where Mount Carmel meets the sea. The diversity of boats reflect the coastal stories: gunboat patrols at Gaza, cruise ships and oil tankers at Haifa, fishing boats at ancient Acre all take to the sea for their different purposes. These waters hold memories both pain-ful and hopeful: Zionist immigrants entered the land via this coast throughout the last century, and in 1948 thousands of Palestinians fled the land from these ports. For readers of the Bible, too, the coast speaks to us of arrivals and departures, of disembarking and setting sail . . .

In ancient times the Philistines, the 'Sea Peoples', occupied the great sea ports of Gaza, Ashdod and Ashkelon along the coastal strip of south-western Canaan, and the Old Testament tells of their conflict with the Israelites in the times of Samson, Samuel, Saul and David. Today, just five miles from Tel Aviv, visitors can enjoy the ancient port of Joppa (Jaffa), which preserves a medieval atmosphere with its narrow streets clinging to the cliffside above the Mediterranean. The cedars of Lebanon for the first Temple floated down to Joppa as rafts, before being taken inland to Jerusalem (2 Chron. 2.16). Jonah took ship from Joppa (Jon. 1.3) when seeking to escape the mission God gave him. Joppa was the main point of arrival for Christian pilgrims to the Holy Land for many centuries, and was predominantly an Arab town until 1948. In the Church of the Resurrection in Jerusalem a remarkable piece of pilgrim graffiti from the fourth century has been found in recent excavations: a rough sketch of a boat, with the words, 'Lord, we made it! We arrived!'

It was at Joppa that Peter received a vision about the mission of the Church which pushed back the boundaries of what he believed possible and opened new frontiers in his understanding of the gospel. As he stood on the housetop overlooking the expansiveness of the sea, he gained a bigger picture of who Jesus came for: not only the Jew but the Gentile. The vastness of the ocean mirrored the message of the vision, as he explained to Cornelius at Caesarea Maritima: 'I truly understand that God shows no partiality, but in every nation anyone who fears him and does what is right is acceptable to him' (Acts 10.34, 35). Here, the veracity of Peter's global vision was confirmed by a second Pentecost (Acts 11.15), declaring that the Good News is for everyone, without distinction – the roots of the world mission of the Church. The magnificent ruins of Caesarea Maritima, the great seaport and harbour built by Herod the Great, still testify to the might and ambition of the Roman client king. From this port, Paul set sail towards the west as 'apostle to the Gentiles' (cf. Acts 18.22; 23.33; 25.4). The mystery and expansiveness of the sea lapping at the shore also impels us, like the first Christians, to rediscover the unbounded mercy and faithfulness of God, as celebrated in Faber's hymn: 'There's a wideness in God's mercy like the wideness of the sea.'

The seas beckon us, the distant skyline summons us. Abba Dorotheus, the sixth-century spiritual writer of Gaza, tells us to keep our eyes on the horizon: 'In every circumstance we must look upwards. Whether someone does good to us or we suffer harm from anyone, we must always look upwards and thank God.'[2] The sea represents the challenge of mission – to go forth. It reminds us of the Great Commission: 'Go therefore and make disciples of all nations' (Matt. 28.19). But as Paul discovered, it is also the place of risk and danger. Paul faces tempestuous winds and a life-threatening storm as his boat drifts across the thunderous sea and meets destruction on the rocks. This shipwreck seems to be the end (Acts 27.41), but in God's purposes becomes the start of an unexpected mission to the island of Malta. And from Malta, Paul continues by ship to Rome itself, 'proclaiming the kingdom of God and teaching about the Lord Jesus Christ' (Acts 28.31).

The sea had always been viewed as a place of danger in the ancient Near East. As far back as the Babylonian Epic of Gilgamesh, the deep was seen as a place of ferocious struggle between divinity and demons, while the Ugarit texts speak of Baal fighting with the sea god Yam. In the Old Testament, God as King of creation wrestles with the dark powers of the ocean, the sea dragons Leviathan and Rahab. This conflict looks back to the primeval chaos before creation (Gen. 1.1) and looks forward to the eschatological victory over the sea-beast (Dan. 7). Psalm 107.23–27 gives us a sense of the dangers . . .

> Some went down to the sea in ships,
> doing business on the mighty waters;
> they saw the deeds of the LORD,
> his wondrous works in the deep.
> For he commanded and raised the stormy wind,
> which lifted up the waves of the sea.
> They mounted up to heaven, they went down to the
>   depths;
> their courage melted away in their calamity;
> they reeled and staggered like drunkards,
> and were at their wits' end.

This was experienced for himself by the prophet Jonah:

You cast me into the deep,
into the heart of the seas,
and the flood surrounded me;
all your waves and your billows passed over me.

(Jon. 2.3)

For Jonah, the sea becomes the place where he discovers the presence of God in a totally unexpected way: the place of danger becomes the place of salvation. Formerly, he had thought that God's presence was localized and limited to the Temple in Jerusalem, and that in fleeing the Holy Land he was escaping the mission God called him to carry out. But he discovers in the waves both God's persistent presence and God's persistent call. God says in the book of Isaiah: 'I have called you by name, you are mine. When you pass through the waters, I will be with you' (Isa. 43.1b, 2a). Vocation and risk seem to be very closely linked.

The challenge of the sea

So, the image of the sea invites us to consider what challenges God might next lay before us. How are we going to live out the questions and challenges of the Holy Land? How are we going to take them into our mission? The maritime metaphor, as we shall see, echoes many of the themes we have touched on in this book, and crystallizes into four major challenges.

Launch into the deep

The biggest question for pilgrims is this: 'Dare I move out of my comfort zone, represented by feet firmly planted on *terra firma*, and venture forth to do things differently?' This challenge resonates with the challenge Jesus gave to Peter at the Sea of Galilee: 'Put out into the deep' (Luke 5.4). The sea invites us to leave behind the security of being on land, and move out into uncharted waters. The shoreline represents the brink of new possibilities. It represents the limit of our own confidence, the edge of our sense of security. But this is a threshold we must cross if we are to live as pilgrims in this world, people on the move, people going places with God.

Catch the wind

The word for 'spirit' derives from the Hebrew *ruach*, meaning 'breath', and from the Greek *pneuma*, which can mean 'wind'. When Luke likens the Spirit of Pentecost to a wind, he does not have in mind a gentle, soothing breeze. Rather, he writes: 'And suddenly from heaven there came a sound like a rush of a violent wind . . . All of them were filled with the Holy Spirit' (Acts 2.2, 4). We are invited to expose our lives to a Spirit who may disturb and discomfort us, as well as empower and energize us. It is a Spirit over which we have no control: 'The wind blows where it chooses, and you hear the sound of it, but you do not know where it comes from or where it goes. So it is with everyone who is born of the Spirit' (John 3.8). As Luke's graphic account of Paul's voyage across the Mediterranean reminds us, the important thing is that we hoist the sails and catch the wind:

> When a moderate south wind began to blow, they thought they could achieve their purpose; so they weighed anchor and began to sail past Crete, close to the shore. But soon a violent wind, called the northeaster, rushed down from Crete. Since the ship was caught and could not be turned with its head to the wind, we gave way to it and were driven.
>
> (Acts 27.13–15)

Later, when they sought to land, 'They cast off the anchors and left them in the sea. At the same time they loosened the ropes that tied the steering-oars; then hoisting the foresail to the wind, they made for the beach' (Acts 27.40). Luke gives us a vivid picture of the need to stay alert to changing wind direction and to follow the signs of the wind's movement. Boats on the sea do not travel in a straight line: they must continually reorientate themselves in order to catch the wind. We must take the risk of exposing ourselves, without guard, to the Spirit of God. As we seek to respond to the challenges of the Holy Land, we realize that, like the local Christians, we need to hear more clearly than ever before what the Spirit is saying to the churches. In solidarity with the often-buffeted Christians of this land, we need to look to God for new reserves of courage: 'God did not give us a spirit of cowardice, but rather a spirit of power and of love and of self-discipline' (2 Tim. 1.7).

Face impossibilities

The image of the sea invites us to confront our fears and anxieties about the future – represented in the uncertain waves. We are crippled into inaction by fear; for example, we worry about the personal cost of getting 'too involved' with political issues or with complex situations, such as are found in the Holy Land. In our personal life we may hang back from a new venture or new expression of ministry thanks to the fear of failure. The sea can represent fear of the unknown: aspects of mission that for us are yet unexplored or unfamiliar waters. We recall the Israelites hovering on the brink of the Red Sea (or Sea of Reeds) in the exodus event. They were faced with the impossibility of crossing the angry and formidable waters, and the risk of being trapped by the pursuing forces of the Pharaoh: 'They said to Moses, "Was it because there were no graves in Egypt that you have taken us away to die in the wilderness?" . . . But Moses said to the people, "Do not be afraid, stand firm, and see the deliverance that the LORD will accomplish for you today"' (Exod. 14.11a, 13a).

To his surprise, the key to salvation was in Moses' own hand, and it was with his action of striking the waters that the miracle of the splitting of the sea occurred. In Jewish spirituality, the 'splitting of the seas' has become a powerful symbol of facing the impossible with God: God makes the impossible possible, but needs men and women to be prepared to plunge into a risky synergy with the divine. In the Christian gospel, Gabriel says to Mary: 'Nothing will be impossible with God'; Mary helps make the impossible happen with her words of surrender: 'Here am I, the servant of the Lord; let it be with me according to your word' (Luke 1.37, 38).

Seventy times in the Bible the words 'Do not be afraid' are repeated. This is a source of encouragement to the Christians of the Middle East, where a strong temptation exists to yield to fatalism or despondency in the face of a failing peace process and the marginalization of Christian minorities. It is easy to give up. In our own personal mission too, we face what seem to be insurmountable problems. The parting of the waters of the sea reminds us that, with God, breakthroughs are possible.[3]

Become navigators and explorers

Israel's coastal waters, thrashed by winter storms and riddled with treacherous currents, are an apt image of the state of today's Holy Land. The sea represents to us the unpredictable conditions of the Middle East and, indeed, life in a postmodern world, where the old and trusted landmarks are fast disappearing. Today's Church needs Christians with a pilgrim heart, navigators who can read the unfolding signs of the times, as much as it needs map readers who can spot the traditional reference points. Paul lists as one of the gifts of the Spirit *kubernetes*: sometimes lamely translated 'administration', it means 'navigation' or 'helmsmanship'. For Paul, the art of discerning the Spirit's movement, the art of recognizing the need of the moment, is akin to the skill of the ship's pilot and steersman who, working collaboratively alongside the captain, the coxswain and the entire crew, will guide the ship in its adventures. In the seventh century John Climacus of Sinai speaks, using this image, of the need for courageous spiritual directors: 'A ship with a good navigator comes safely to port, God willing.'[4]

The image of navigation was central to the experience of the Celtic Christians, who had lively traditions of peregrination and voyaging on the rough seas around Ireland and Scotland. They were motivated by a desire both to spread the gospel and to discover God's providence in the deep. The sixth-century *Voyage of St Brendan* tells us:

> St Brendan then embarked, and they set sail . . . They had a fair wind, and therefore no labour, only to keep the sails properly set; but after twelve days the wind fell to a dead calm, and they had to labour at the oars until their strength was nearly exhausted. Then St Brendan would encourage and exhort them: 'Fear not, brothers, for our God will be unto us a helper, a mariner, and a pilot; take in the oars and helm,

keep the sails set, and may God do unto us, His servants and His little vessel, as He wills.'[5]

The ancient liturgy of the Ethiopian Church, heard in Jerusalem daily at the Church of the Resurrection, also calls on God as pilot:

> Pilot of the soul, leader of righteousness, refuge of salvation, grant us Lord to have eyes trained so that we may always see you, and ears to hear only your Word ... Grant us a pure heart so that we may always appreciate your goodness, you kind one and lover of the world!

'He is going *ahead of you* to Galilee; there you will see him' (Mark 16.7). The words of the angel to the fearful women at the empty tomb on Easter Day alert them to where the Risen One is waiting for them. In Mark's perspective 'Galilee' represents the place of mission – as Matthew reminds us, it is 'on the road by the sea, across the Jordan, Galilee of the Gentiles' (Matt. 4.15). Mark tells us that the Risen Christ will meet us in the place of mission; moreover he is going on before us, ahead of us, to prepare the way. Like Jonah of old, we realize that it is time to disembark – God has given us a mission to fulfil. Our prayer will be that of the prophet: 'But the earth will be filled with the knowledge of the glory of the LORD, as the waters cover the sea' (Hab. 2.14).

In this book I have invited you to traverse the landscape of the Holy Land, and to discern its questions. You have been invited not only to explore the physical terrain, ancient and contemporary, but also the spiritual, interior world to which it so powerfully points.

We have explored issues of home, identity and holiness. The rocks required us to wrestle with the dilemmas involved in memory and forgiveness. The depths drew us into the mystery of God's workings, while the heights asked us to let go and expose ourselves unreservedly to the elements, spiritual and physical. The desert echoed this theme as it summoned us to naked encounter with God, while gardens, rather than soothing the soul, took us into the heart of the spiritual and physical struggle. Walls and roads led us to break free from confinement and experience the unpredictable. Waters plunged us into questions about the sharing of resources and contemporary vocation.

The terrain of the Holy Land has posed its inescapable questions. But ultimately the biblical landscape invites us to be explorers of the sacred spaces in our own lives and in our own contexts. It summons us to a risky, adventurous discipleship and to a courageous mission on the soil of our own lands.

Questions for reflection

1 What specific courses of action are open to you through which you can show support to those who struggle in the Holy Land today? In particular, how can you support the Christian community at this time?

2 What fears do you face as you move into the future? What kinds of courage do you need most?

3 In the light of this book, do you sense that there are ways in which you should be moving forward in your discipleship and ministry?

4 How would you express the mission to which the Risen Christ is calling you?

5 How can you live as a pilgrim in your own land and setting?

For further reading

J. D. Clift and B. Wallace, *The Archetype of Pilgrimage: Outer Action with Inner Meanings* (New York: Paulist Press, 1996)

J. G. Davies, *Pilgrimage Yesterday and Today: Why? Where? How?* (London: SCM, 1988)

J. Ortberg, *If You Want to Walk on Water, You've Got to Get Out of the Boat* (Grand Rapids, MI: Zondervan, 2001)

P. J. Palmer, *Let Your Life Speak: Listening for the Voice of Vocation* (San Francisco: Jossey-Bass, 1999)

M. Silf, *At Sea with God: A Spiritual Guidebook to the Heart and Soul* (Notre Dame, IN: Ave Maria Press, 2008)

Notes

1 The city's questions

1 Report of Ir Amin Foundation, reported in *Ha'aretz*, 14 November 2005. Dropout rates are increasing, too: more than 50 per cent of Palestinian boys who start school in Jerusalem fail to complete their studies.

2 Palestinian Central Bureau of Statistics, quoted in J. Gough, 'The Situation of Children in the Occupied Palestinian Territory', *This Week in Palestine*, 154, February 2011.

3 Ilan Pappe, *The Ethnic Cleansing of Palestine* (Oxford: Oneworld, 2007).

4 See, for example, A. Qleibo, *Before the Mountains Disappear: An Ethnographic Chronicle of the Modern Palestinians* (Jerusalem: Kloreus, 1992).

5 See, for example, J. D. Crossan, *Jesus: A Revolutionary Biography* (San Francisco: HarperCollins, 1995).

6 M. Crosby, *House of Disciples: Church, Economics, and Justice in Matthew* (New York: Orbis Books, 1988).

2 The land's questions

1 For example, at Nazareth the altar's marker says, *Verbum caro hic factum est*: 'Here the Word became flesh.'

2 A. Pacini, *Socio-Political and Community Dynamics of Arab Christians in Jordan, Israel, and the Autonomous Palestinian Territories* (Oxford: Clarendon Press, 1998), p. 282.

3 The three camps are Dheisheh, Aida and Al-Azzeh.

4 Liberation theology has opened our eyes to the ways in which God reveals his kingdom and his presence precisely through the poor. See, for example, L. Boff, *Jesus Christ Liberator: A Critical Christology For Our Times* (New York: Orbis, 1978).

5 From <www.motherteresacause.info>.

6 St John Chrysostom, Homily 50, *On the Gospel of Matthew*, 3–4.

7 For more on *tikkun* see G. G. Scholem, *Major Trends in Jewish Mysticism* (London: Thames & Hudson, 1955); A. Green (ed.), *Jewish*

Spirituality: From the Sixteenth-Century Revival to the Present (London: SCM, 1988).

3 The river's questions

1 The State, however, does not follow this definition: Israeli citizenship is denied to those who are Jewish by birth or blood but have converted to another faith. For example, Jews who have become Messianic Christians are considered to have forfeited their Jewishness.
2 See United Nations data, <www.unhcr.org>.
3 O. Cullmann, *Christology of the New Testament* (London: SCM, 1963), p. 97.
4 J. Ziesler, *Paul's Letter to the Romans* (London: SCM, 1993), p. 162.
5 *Common Worship: Christian Initiation* (London: Church House Publishing, 2006). Prayer taken from *Common Worship: Christian Initiation* © The Archbishops' Council 2006. Used by permission: <copyright@churchofengland.org>.

4 The cave's questions

1 S. Gibson, *The Final Days of Jesus: The Archaeological Evidence* (New York: HarperOne, 2009).
2 See M. Biddle, *The Tomb of Christ* (Stroud: Sutton Publishing, 1999).
3 *Life of Constantine*, quoted in P. W. L. Walker, *Holy City, Holy Places?* (Oxford: Clarendon Press, 1990), p. 186.
4 H. Whybrew, *Risen with Christ* (London: SPCK, 2001), p. 28. Reproduced by permission.
5 Holy Transfiguration Monastery, *The Pentecostarion* (Boston, MA: Holy Transfiguration Monastery, 1990), p. 34. Copyright © 1990, Holy Transfiguration Monastery, Brookline, MA, used by permission. All rights reserved.
6 For a critique of the ascent model, see M. Miles, *The Image and Practice of Holiness* (London: SCM, 1989).
7 N. G. Cosby, *By Grace Transformed: Christianity for a New Millennium* (New York: Crossroad, 1998), p. 31.
8 P. Tillich, *The Shaking of the Foundations* (New York: Charles Scribner & Sons, 1955), p. 55.
9 R. Foster, *Celebration of Discipline* (San Francisco: Harper, 1988), p. 1.
10 K. Kavanaugh and O. Rodriguez (trans.), *The Collected Works of St. John of the Cross* (Washington: Institute of Carmelite Studies, 1991), p. 114. From *The Collected Works of St. John of the Cross*, translated

by Kieran Kavanaugh and Otilio Rodriguez. Copyright © 1964, 1979, 1991 by Washington Province of Discalced Carmelites, ICS Publications, 2131 Lincoln Road, N.E., Washington, DC 20002-1199, U.S.A., <www.icspublications.org>, used with permission. All rights reserved.

11 See, for example, J. D. Crossan, *Jesus: A Revolutionary Biography* (San Francisco: HarperCollins, 1995).

12 Israeli Jews face their own darkness too, as we shall consider: unhealed wounds from the Holocaust, and constant fear and anxiety about security and safety.

13 *Pentecostarion*, p. 29. Copyright © 1990, Holy Transfiguration Monastery, Brookline, MA, used by permission. All rights reserved.

5 The rock's questions

1 M. Halwachs, *On Collective Memory* (Chicago: University of Chicago Press, 1992).

2 J. B. Metz, *Faith in History and Society* (New York: Herder & Herder, 2007), p. 105. In Metz's perspective dangerous memory is inseparable from 'eschatological remembrance', which in recalling the *memoria resurrectionis* as well as the *memoria passionis* is open to a future hope where within God's reign or kingdom freedom triumphs: 'In the memory of his suffering it is the future of freedom that is being remembered' (p. 107).

3 G. Müller-Fahrenholz, *The Art of Forgiveness: Theological Reflections on Healing and Reconciliation* (Geneva: World Council of Churches, 1997), p. 48.

4 M. H. Ellis, *Revolutionary Forgiveness* (Waco, TX: Baylor University Press, 2000), p. 281.

5 Ellis, *Revolutionary Forgiveness*, p. 276.

6 C. Heyward, quoted in M. H. Ellis, *Beyond Innocence and Redemption: Confronting the Holocaust and Israeli Power* (San Francisco: Harper & Row, 1990), p. 182.

7 N. Ateek, *Justice and Only Justice: A Palestinian Theology of Liberation* (Maryknoll, NY: Orbis, 1989), p. 186.

8 In Islam, the practice of throwing stones at the Devil (at pillars, latterly walls, representing Satan), during the *hajj* or pilgrimage to Mecca, has become an important expression of 'the repudiation of one's self' (*al-Nafs al-Amarah*, literally 'the internal despot'). Each pilgrim is required to throw 49 stones – no easy task! It can represent the casting aside of one's low desires and wishes, a sense of release and resolve to overcome evil.

9 It evokes Toplady's hymn:

> Rock of Ages, cleft for me,
> let me hide myself in Thee.
> Let the water and the blood
> from Thy wounded side which flowed
> be of sin the double cure,
> cleanse me from its guilt and power.

10 See Anglican-Roman Catholic International Commission, *The Final Report* (London: CTS/SPCK, 1982), p. 14.
11 N. Ateek, *Contemporary Way of the Cross* (Jerusalem: Sabeel Ecumenical Liberation Centre, 2005).
12 N. Ward, *The Use of Praying* (London: Epworth Press, 1967).
13 E. Underhill, *Life as Prayer* (London: Mowbray, 1946), p. 59.
14 L. Boff, *Way of the Cross – Way of Justice* (New York: Orbis, 1980).

6 The mountain's questions

1 A. J. Malherbe and E. Ferguson (trans.), *Gregory of Nyssa: the Life of Moses* (New York: Paulist Press, 1978), p. 95.
2 'The Mystical Theology', 1, in C. Luibheid (trans.), *Pseudo-Dionysius: the Complete Works* (New York: Paulist Press, 1987), p. 135.
3 V. Lossky, *The Mystical Theology of the Eastern Church* (London: James Clarke, 1957), p. 223.
4 C. Wolters (trans.), *The Cloud of Unknowing* (London: Penguin, 1976), pp. 53, 54. For a more recent translation see J. Walsh (trans.), *The Cloud of Unknowing* (New York: Paulist Press, 1981).
5 Source: <www.palestinemonitor.org>.
6 See J. D. Crossan, *God and Empire* (San Francisco: HarperOne, 2007).
7 S. R. Sizer, 'An Alternative Theology of the Holy Land: A Critique of Christian Zionism', *The Churchman* 133:2 (1999).

7 The lake's questions

1 Three million Palestinians use 250 million cubic metres a year, while six million Israelis use 2,000 million cubic metres, according to <www.palestinemonitor.org>.
2 Quoted in J. Meyendorff, *St Gregory Palamas and Orthodox Spirituality* (New York: St Vladimir's Seminary Press, 1974), p. 49.
3 Teresa of Avila, *Interior Castle*, trans. by E. A. Peers (London: Sheed & Ward, 1974), p. 37.

4 P. W. L. Walker, *Jesus and His World* (Oxford: Lion Publishing, 2003), p. 30.

8 The garden's questions

1 W. C. Chittick, 'Eschatology', in S. H. Nasr, *Islamic Spirituality: Foundations* (London: SCM, 1989), p. 394.

2 Attributed to Baba Tahir of Hamadan (11th century), in Nasr, *Islamic Spirituality*, p. 400.

3 Attributed to Persian poet Sana'i, in Nasr, *Islamic Spirituality*, p. 397.

4 Source: <www.mamillacampaign.org>.

5 See A. Khalidi, 'The Mamilla Cemetery: A Buried History', in *Jerusalem Quarterly* 37 (Spring 2009), at <www.jerusalemquarterly.org>.

6 W. L. Lane, *Hebrews: A Call to Commitment* (Peabody, MA: Hendrickson, 1985), p. 81.

7 M. Basilea Schlink, *The Holy Land Today* (London: Marshall, Morgan & Scott, 1975), p. 65.

8 Look at Psalms 10, 74, 79, 106 (community laments) and Psalms 13, 42, 73 (individual struggles).

9 The desert's questions

1 R. M. Rice (trans.), *Lives of the Monks of Palestine by Cyril of Scythopolis* (Kalamazoo, MI: Cistercian Publicans, 1991), p. 11.

2 All the quotations from Basil are from Letter 2, in G. Barrois (trans.), *The Fathers Speak* (New York: St Vladimir's Seminary Press, 1986).

3 B. Ward, *The Sayings of the Desert Fathers* (Oxford: Mowbray, 1975), p. 131.

4 T. Merton, *The Wisdom of the Desert* (Boston, MA and London: Shambhala, 1960), pp. 4, 7.

5 H. Nouwen, *The Way of the Heart* (London: Darton, Longman & Todd, 1987), pp. 27, 32.

6 Jerome, *Letter to Heliodorus*.

7 G. A. Maloney, *Intoxicated with God: The Fifty Spiritual Homilies of Macarius* (New Jersey: Dimension Books, 1978), p. 33.

10 The wall's questions

1 For UN reports on the Separation Barrier see <www.ochaopt.org>.

2 J. P. Meier, *A Marginal Jew: Rethinking the Historical Jesus* (New York: Doubleday, 1991); B. J. Malina, *The New Testament World:*

Insights from Cultural Anthropology (Louisville, KY: John Knox Press, 1981).

3 R. Horsley, *Jesus and Empire: The Kingdom of God and the New World Disorder* (Minneapolis, MN: Fortress Press, 2002).

11 The road's questions

1 The phrase comes from G. Gutierrez, *A Theology of Liberation* (London: SCM, 1988).
2 C. P. Thiede, *The Emmaus Mystery: Discovering Evidence for the Risen Christ* (London: Continuum, 2005).

12 The sea's questions

1 *The Guardian*, 27 July 2010.
2 'St Abba Dorotheus: Directions on Spiritual Training', in E. Kadloubovsky and G. E. H. Palmer (trans.), *Early Fathers from the Philokalia* (Faber & Faber, London, 1969), p. 166.
3 For organizations supporting the Christians of the Holy Land, contact Jerusalem and the Middle East Church Association (<www.jmeca.org>); Sabeel, the centre for Palestinian liberation theology and reconciliation (<www.friendsofsabeel.org.uk>); the Amos Trust (<www.amostrust.org>); the Barnabas Fund (<www.barnabasfund.org>); St George's College Jerusalem (<www.sgcjerusalem.org>).
4 C. Luibheid and N. Russell (trans.), *John Climacus: The Ladder of Divine Ascent* (New York: Paulist Press, 1982), p. 259.
5 D. O'Donoghue (trans.), *Voyage of St Brendan the Abbot*, from <www.lamp.ac.uk/celtic/elibrary>.